DB2 11:
The Database
for Big Data & Analytics

Cristian Molaro

Surekha Parekh

Terry Purcell

Julian Stuhler

MC PRESS

MC Press Online, LLC

Boise, ID 83703 USA

DB2 11: The Database for Big Data and Analytics
Cristian Molaro, Surekha Parekh, Terry Purcell, and Julian Stuhler

First Edition
First Printing—October 2013

MC Press offers excellent discounts on this book when ordered in quantity for bulk purchases or special sales, which may include custom covers and content particular to your business, training goals, marketing focus, and branding interest.

Corporate Offices:
MC Press Online, LLC
3695 W. Quail Heights Court
Boise, ID 83703-3861 USA
www.mc-store.com

Sales and Customer Service:
service@mcpressonline.com
(208) 629-7275 ext. 500

ISBN: 978-1-58347-385-6

Contents

About the Authors

Cristian Molaro (*cristian@molaro.be*) is an independent DB2 specialist and IBM Gold Consultant focused on DB2 for z/OS administration and performance. He was recognized as an IBM Champion in 2009, 2010, 2011, 2012, and 2013. Cristian has presented papers at several international conferences and local user groups in Europe and North America and is coauthor of eight IBM Redbooks related to DB2, including *DB2 11 for z/OS Technical Overview*. A recipient of the merit badge "Platinum IBM Redbook Author," Cristian is part of the IDUG EMEA Conference Planning Committee and chairman of the DB2 LUW User Group BeLux. He was recognized by IBM as Top EMEA Consultant at the IDUG EMEA 2011 DB2 Tech Conference in Prague.

Julian Stuhler (*julian.stuhler@triton.co.uk*) is a Principal Consultant with Triton Consulting, a U.K. company providing DB2 consultancy, education, software, and managed services to clients throughout Europe. He has more than 25 years of relational database experience, working for clients in the insurance, telecom, banking, financial services, and manufacturing sectors. Julian has lectured widely on DB2 subjects, in both the United Kingdom and Europe, and he won the Best Overall Speaker award at the 2000 IDUG European Conference. Julian coauthored an IBM Redbook on Java stored procedures and contributes frequently to industry publications such as *IDUG Solutions Journal* and *Database Journal*. Julian is an IBM DB2 Gold Consultant, Past-President of the IDUG Board of Directors, and an IBM Champion.

Surekha Parekh (*surekhaparekh@uk.ibm.com*) is IBM's World-Wide Marketing Program Director for DB2 for z/OS. She also leads the Social Media Strategy for Information Management on System z. Surekha is responsible for market strategy and planning of DB2 on System z and for building social media communities for Information Management System z. Based in Warwick, United Kingdom, Surekha is a passionate marketer with proven results. She has more than 27 years of business experience and is passionate about Information Management. Surekha represents IBM on the IDUG committee. IDUG is an independent DB2 user group with more than 16,000 members in more than 100 countries.

Terry Purcell (*tpurcel@us.ibm.com*) is a Senior Technical Staff Member, DB2 Development, with the IBM Silicon Valley Lab, where he is lead designer for the DB2 for z/OS Optimizer. Terry has two decades of experience with DB2 in database administration and application development as a customer, consultant, and DB2 developer.

Introduction

IBM DB2 11:
The Database for Big Data and Critical Business Analytics

by Surekha Parekh

I joined the DB2 business in 2008, just after the launch of IBM® DB2 9 for z/OS®. A lot has changed in the World of Data since then. In fact, a lot has changed in the world of business and information technology—and the changes are going to continue.

There has been an enormous explosion of data: 90 percent of the world's data has been created over the past two years![1] We have also seen a rapid growth in the volume, variety, and velocity of data due to the explosion of smart devices, mobile applications, cloud computing, and social media. New technology innovations, hunger for data, and the thirst for business analytics signal that we are entering a new era of computing—**Smarter Computing**—the **era of Insight for Discovery**.

Every second[2], there are. . .

- 684,478 items shared on Facebook
- 100,000 tweets
- 2 million Google search queries
- 1 new member joining LinkedIn
- 58 hours of video uploaded to YouTube

Much of this data growth has been in unstructured data; however, IDC estimates that by 2020, business transactions on the Internet—business-to-business and business-to-consumer—will reach **450 billion per day**[3]. This phenomenon of data explosion is called **big data**, and smart organizations are looking for innovative ways to collect, analyze, and turn this data into actionable insights and make predictions.

Big data is changing our world, the world of our children. Can you imagine a world where you can predict chronic illnesses such as cancer, heart disease, Parkinson's disease, and diabetes before they happen? That is the world at our fingertips. Through the analysis of these data mountains, it will become possible not only to analyze critical illnesses before they occur but to improve business efficiencies. Every industry, every organization, every government, and every individual will be impacted by this data revolution. Innovative companies know that software is the way not only to improve business efficiencies but also to differentiate products and services from the competition and survive.

Big data is of particular concern when it comes to information security because it puts private information at risk. The cost per incident for a security breach is on average $5.4M[4]. Today's organizations are challenged to ensure that their business data is secure. According to IBM, more than 80 percent of corporate data resides on mainframes, and common estimates suggest that 85 percent of all business transactions are processed by mainframes today[5]. This positions DB2 11 for z/OS as the ideal database for big data and critical analytics in the new era of computing. It is the only proven, secure, and cost-effective platform trusted by top banks, insurance companies, and retailers.

The objective of this book is to give our customers insight into DB2 11, which was announced on October 1, 2013. Everyone is talking about DB2 11. Many of our Early Support Program customers have been testing this product and are seeing some incredible results! Our customers and business partners around the world are very enthusiastic.

So what's new in DB2 11 that is causing so much excitement? Here is a quick summary of some of the exciting new features and business benefits of DB2 11, about which this book will give you deeper insight:

- Even more out-of-the-box CPU savings

  - 10 percent complex OLTP
  - 10 percent update intensive batch
  - 40 percent queries
  - 25 percent uncompressed tables and 40% compressed tables

- Enhanced resiliency

  - Fewer planned outages, fewer REORGs, faster recovery
  - Cost-effective archiving, access warm/cold data in single query

- Business-critical analytics

  - DB2 Analytics Accelerator performance enhancements
  - Big data integration
  - In-transaction real-time scoring
  - Advanced QMF analytic capabilities with mobile support

- Simpler, faster upgrades for faster ROI

  - 16x faster catalog migration
  - Protection from incompatible changes
  - Repeatable testing with real workloads and integrated cloning

The book is segmented into two parts. The first part is all about the business value of DB2 11 for z/OS and explains the unmatched efficiency for big data and analytics. This section also includes short papers on the DB2 11 Optimizer and the business value of IBM tools and utilities. The second section focuses more on DB2 and System z[®] and how

DB2 for z/OS can reduce the total cost of ownership for organizations. With the enormous explosion of data, this is more critical now than ever before.

We hope you find this book as valuable as our previous versions. Many thanks.

Surekha Parekh

World-Wide Marketing Program Director – DB2 for z/OS

http://www.linkedin.com/in/surekhaparekh

Notes

1. Dan Vesset at al. *Worldwide Big Data Technology and Services 2012–2015 Forecast* (IDC, March 7, 2012).

2. 2013 digital statistics from MistMedia, Dublin, Ireland.

3. David Reinsel and John Gantz. *The Digital Universe in 2020: Big Data, Bigger Digital Shadows, and Biggest Growth in the Far East* (IDC, December 2012).

4. Ponemon Institute, annual data breach report, June 2013.

5. http://www.memorableurl.com/2012/11/whats-next-cloud-applicationson-a-mainframe.html

DB2 11 for z/OS:
Unmatched Efficiency
for Big Data and Analytics

by Julian Stuhler

Few IT professionals can have missed the big data phenomenon that has manifested itself in recent years. Industry publications and IT analysts have devoted a huge percentage of their output to the subject (creating a big data challenge all their own in the process). There can be little doubt that the advent of new technologies and methods of customer and business interaction have created unique challenges for organizations wishing to create actionable insight from very large amounts of unstructured data. Innovative tools and techniques have been developed to cope with these "big data" challenges (and indeed some of them are discussed in this paper, in the "Hadoop and Big Data Support" section).

However, beyond this somewhat narrow definition of big data, many organizations have been dealing with the challenges of processing, maintaining, and analyzing ever-increasing amounts of more traditionally structured data for many years. The inherent scalability and resilience of IBM® DB2® for z/OS® and the underlying System z® platform have proven to be a compelling combination for such applications, and IBM continues to invest in extending DB2's capabilities with each new release.

From transparent archiving to greater in-memory scalability through the use of 2 GB page frames, DB2 11 for z/OS, the latest release of IBM's flagship database, contains many new features specifically designed to help customers to address the challenges of managing traditional big data. A wealth of material exists on the technical changes within DB2 11, but finding descriptions of how those new features will improve your business results can be a challenge. The main body of this paper provides a high-level overview of the major new features from an IT executive's perspective, with emphasis on the under-lying business value that DB2 11 can deliver.

This is the fourth paper in this series, with previous editions highlighting the business value offered by DB2 for z/OS V8.1, DB2 9 for z/OS, and DB2 10 for z/OS:

- *DB2 for z/OS 8.1: Driving Business Value* (J. Stuhler, Triton Consulting, 2004)
- *DB2 9 for z/OS: Data on Demand* (J. Stuhler, Triton Consulting, 2007)
- *DB2 10 for z/OS: A Smarter Database for a Smarter Planet* (J. Stuhler, Triton Consulting, 2010)

NOTE: Throughout the remainder of this document, all references to "DB2 9," "DB2 10," and "DB2 11" refer to the relevant release of IBM DB2 for z/OS.

DB2 11 for z/OS: The Database for Big Data and Analytics

In this section, we take a detailed look at the major features of DB2 11 for z/OS and see how many of IBM's most innovative enterprise customers plan to use them to deliver an enhanced IT service to the business. Many of these enhancements can deliver benefits "out of the box," with little or no effort required to begin exploiting them, reducing the time-to-value for a DB2 11 upgrade. See "DB2 11 New Features by Implementation Effort" (opposite) for a breakdown of the effort required to exploit each new feature.

This section is organized around the key DB2 11 themes:

- **Efficiency.** Reducing cost and improving productivity
- **Resilience.** Improving availability and data security
- **Business analytics.** Enhanced query and reporting

Efficiency

Even in the most favorable economic climate, businesses need to control costs and increase efficiency to improve their bottom line. In today's increasingly challenging business environment, this continues to be a key factor for the survival and success of enterprises of all sizes.

This section examines the major DB2 11 enhancements that are aimed at delivering the highest efficiency for core IT systems that rely on DB2, a key design objective for the new release. These features can help reduce ongoing operational costs, improve developer and DBA productivity, and enhance customer experience by increasing performance and delivering a more responsive application.

CPU Reductions

Most DB2 for z/OS customers operate on a CPU usage-based charging model, so any increases or decreases in the amount of CPU required to run DB2 applications can have a direct and very significant impact on overall operational costs.

Traditionally, IBM has tried to limit the additional CPU cost of adding new functionality into each release, keeping the net CPU impact below 5 percent. The move to a 64-bit computing platform in DB2 for z/OS Version 8 was an exception to this rule and introduced some significant processing overheads that resulted in many customers experiencing net CPU increases of 5 to 10 percent following the upgrade.

DB2 9 for z/OS helped to redress the balance somewhat by delivering modest CPU improvements for many large customers, but the advent of DB2 10 completely changed the picture. IBM delivered the most aggressive performance improvements of any DB2 release in the past 20 years, with many customers seeing net CPU savings of 5 to 10 percent or more in their traditional DB2 online transaction processing (OLTP) workload without any application changes being required.[1] Unsurprisingly, these savings proved to be very popular and are consistently quoted as being one of the major reasons for customers to upgrade to DB2 10.

DB2 11 New Features by Implementation Effort

One of the most compelling features of DB2 11 is the number of enhancements that can deliver business benefit with little or no change being required to existing applications. The lists below categorize the covered DB2 11 features in this paper according to the amount of effort required to exploit them:

Minor Implementation Effort – Immediate. These features are available immediately after upgrading to DB2 11, with no database or application changes required. A REBIND may be required.

Minor Implementation Effort – Deferred. These features do not require any database or application changes but will be available only after the DB2 system has been placed in New Function Mode.

Significant Database/System Changes Required. These features require some changes to be made to DB2 objects and structures (typically by the DBA), but no application changes. These changes are typically quicker and less expensive to implement/test than application changes.

Significant Application Changes Required. These enhancements require some degree of application change in order to implement and will therefore be the most expensive to implement and test.

Minor Implementation Effort – Immediate
CPU reductions
Application compatibility
pureXML enhancements
Optimizer and query performance improvements
Data sharing performance enhancements
Enhanced dynamic schema change (some features)
BIND/REBIND enhancements

Minor Implementation Effort – Deferred
zEC12 exploitation (also requires DB2 to be running on a zEC12-class server)
Temporal data enhancements
Utility enhancements
Enhanced dynamic schema change (some features)

Significant Database/System Changes Required
Java stored procedure enhancements
Extended log record addressing
Security enhancements

Significant Application Changes Required
Transparent archiving
Global variables
Variable arrays
SQL aggregation improvements
Hadoop and big data support

IBM has further developed the CPU reduction theme within DB2 11, with initial savings of up to 5 percent expected for customers running simple OLTP workloads. Significantly higher savings are possible for complex OLTP and query workloads, as discussed below. Because these improvements are due to internal DB2 code optimization, they are available in DB2 11 Conversion Mode, without the need for any application changes. Additional CPU savings are possible once customers begin to use some of the other DB2 11 enhancements that require application change, as described elsewhere in this section.

Some workloads will benefit more than others from the performance enhancements offered by DB2 11. Figure 1 breaks down the anticipated CPU savings by workload type.

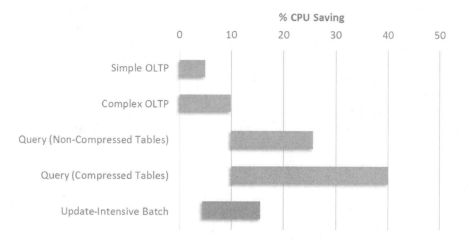

Figure 1: DB2 11 CM vs. DB2 10 NFM – Expected CPU savings by workload type

The most significant benefits are expected to be seen within query workloads. Complex reporting queries can see up to 25 percent savings for uncompressed tables and up to 40 percent for queries on compressed tables. Reporting queries with heavy sort processing may also see additional DB2 CPU savings.

Traditional OLTP workloads are also likely to benefit from the efficiency enhancements in DB2 11. Savings of up to 5 percent are expected for simple OLTP,[2] with reductions of up to 10 percent for more complex transactions. Finally, update-intensive batch workloads may enjoy CPU reductions of 5 to 15 percent.

Figures 2 and 3 depict some actual observed CPU reductions for sample workloads, run as part of IBM's internal performance testing for the new release. These figures are broadly in line with the high-level expectations detailed above.

The overall out-of-the-box CPU savings within DB2 11 are expected to be one of the major factors supporting the business case for upgrading to the new release.

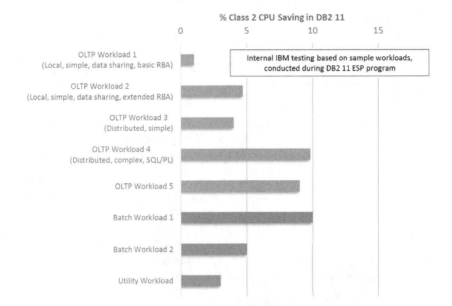

Figure 2: DB2 11 CM vs. DB2 10 NFM – Sample OLTP/batch CPU savings

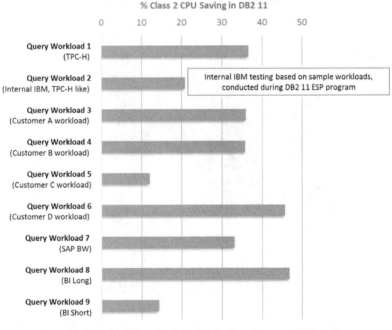

Figure 3: DB2 11 CM vs. DB2 10 NFM – Sample query CPU savings

zEC12 Exploitation

In August 2012, IBM announced the latest-generation IBM zEnterprise® EC12 (zEC12) enterprise servers, with up to 101 configurable processors per server, each running at an industry-leading 5.5 GHz. In addition to an impressive list of general performance and capacity improvements over the previous-generation z196 enterprise servers, the zEC12 models include a number of features that DB2 11 will specifically exploit.

2 GB page frames. DB2 10 for z/OS introduced support for 1 MB "large page frames," an enhancement designed to reduce processing overheads for very large DB2 buffer pools by letting z/OS manage the underlying storage in fewer 1 MB pieces rather than many more 4 KB pieces (Figure 4).

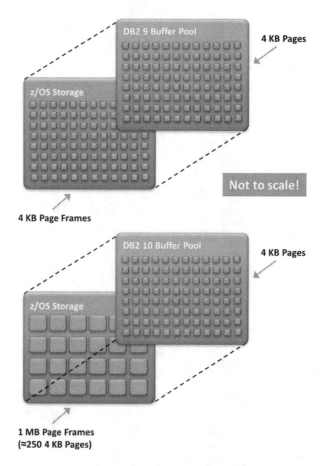

Figure 4: DB2 10 large page frame enhancement

Many customers with larger DB2 buffer pools were able to achieve CPU savings of up to 4 percent by exploiting this capability. However, as memory prices fall and workloads increase, DB2 buffer pools continue to increase in size, and the overheads of managing even the larger 1 MB page frames start to become significant.

In recognition of these trends, when running on an zEC12 server DB2 11 will support even larger 2 GB page frames, each of which will map onto more than half a million 4 KB pages (Figure 5).

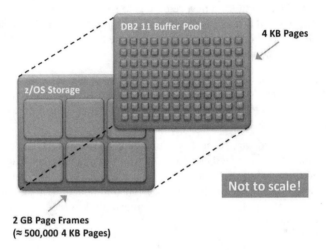

Figure 5: DB2 11 large page frame enhancement

Those customers using very large DB2 buffer pools will see further CPU reductions by moving to 2 GB page frames. Other sites may not have sufficiently large pools for 1 MB page frames to be a significant limitation today, but that situation will undoubtedly change in the future as buffer pool sizes continue to grow. By moving early to support 2 GB page frames, IBM has recognized and eliminated an important future scalability issue.

DB2 code using large page frames. As discussed in the previous section, DB2 10 and DB2 11 have exploited 1 MB and 2 GB large page frames to allow more efficient handling of large buffer pools. However, despite the extensive use of large memory objects in the past few releases of DB2, the storage used for DB2 code (as opposed to the data held in buffer pools) remained backed by standard 4 KB page frames.

DB2 11 is able to utilize large page frames for DB2 code objects and log output buffers, in addition to buffer pools. This enhancement reduces the z/OS overheads associated with DB2 code objects, lowering CPU consumption and operational costs. (Support for running DB2 code in large page frames requires z/OS 2.1.)

Application Compatibility

Many new releases of DB2 introduce enhancements or new features that require application and/or SQL code to be changed. These include additional SQL reserved words, changes to DB2 behavior or processing and even changes to SQL return codes. Although IBM tries to minimize these "incompatible changes," they cannot always be avoided. They may be required in order to ensure that DB2 adheres to evolving SQL standards, to support new functionality, or perhaps to address an earlier defect in the DB2 code.

A major part of planning for a new release is to analyze the impact of these incompatible changes and arrange for the necessary amendments to be made to DB2 application code so it will continue to work as designed under the new release. This situation poses some challenges for DB2 customers:

- Analysis of the impact of incompatible changes can be difficult, time consuming, and error-prone. Missing one or more of the required changes may result in application outages when DB2 is upgraded (or worse, the application may continue to work but return unexpected results).

- Finding the necessary resources to undertake any required remedial work (and scheduling the associated change slots) can be expensive and require significant elapsed time. All of the changes within a given subsystem or data sharing group must be completed before the upgrade can commence, so a lack of resources within a single application team could impact the upgrade schedule for the entire environment.

Figure 6 depicts these challenges.

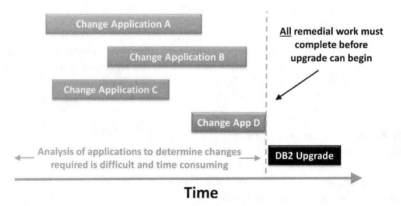

Figure 6: Application compatibility issues

To address these issues and allow customers to upgrade their DB2 systems with less effort and risk, IBM has introduced some new capabilities in DB2 11 for z/OS that remove the hard dependency on all remedial work being conducted before a version upgrade and allow the impact of incompatible changes to be more easily assessed. Figure 7 summarizes these enhancements.

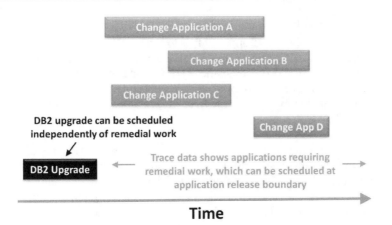

Figure 7: DB2 11 application compatibility feature

When upgrading to DB2 11, customers will be able to defer some or all of the remedial work for incompatible SQL DML and XML changes and allow the DBA or developer to request that DB2 behaves the same as it did for DB2 10 on an application-by-application basis. Although the remedial work will still need to be done at some point, DBAs and developers are now free to schedule it a later date and in a more manageable, staged fashion that conforms to the requirements of the business (e.g., as part of a regular application release). In the meantime, other applications can benefit from the enhancements in the new release.

Furthermore, IBM has provided additional trace data in DB2 11 that can identify applications using incompatible SQL and XML statements after the version upgrade has been implemented. This will enable DBAs and developers to identify applications requiring remedial work much more efficiently, and with less risk of some being accidentally missed.

Because the intention of this feature is to allow more manageable implementation of remedial work, not to defer it work indefinitely, this capability is limited in the number of previously supported releases. In DB2 11, this feature provides backwards compatibility only for DB2 10. Beyond DB2 11, compatibility for up two previous releases will be provided. This means that the release following DB2 11 will support both DB2 10 and DB2 11 compatibility, thereby allowing plenty of time for any remedial work to be undertaken.

By breaking the hard dependency on performing all remedial work prior to an upgrade and providing valuable tools to assist with the identification of that work, the DB2 Application Compatibility feature addresses many of the issues associated with handling incompatible changes in each new DB2 release. This capability should be a huge benefit to customers struggling to line up the necessary application development/ DBA resources to address incompatible changes prior to DB2 11 implementation.

Transparent Archiving

A common requirement for any IT application is to be able to archive old or less frequently accessed data. Regulatory restrictions may require data to be retained for many years, but access frequency tends to drop off dramatically as the data ages). Moving older data to a separate archive can reduce the cost of retrieving and maintaining more frequently used data and allow slower but much less expensive storage devices to be used.

Unfortunately, archiving is usually one of the last areas to be considered and developed for a new application, and it is therefore common to see it deferred until later code releases (or bypassed completely) if time and/or funding is scarce. Even when it is properly implemented, many hundreds of person-hours can be spent in implementing and testing the necessary logic to allow older data to be placed automatically in the archive store while ensuring that the application retains access to it when required.

DB2 11 introduces some new features to simplify application development for archiving data, as well as improve consistency between applications and reduce the amount of time required for testing. When defining the operational DB2 table, the DBA also defines an identical archive table and connects the two via an ALTER TABLE ... ENABLE ARCHIVE statement. Any subsequent changes to the operational table (e.g., adding a column) will automatically be made to the archive table so they remain in step. If required, the archive table can be placed on older, cheaper disk devices, with the more frequently accessed operational data residing on faster storage.

Once an archiving relationship has been defined, DB2 can automatically and transparently handle archiving and retrieval of data from the operational and archive tables. The new DB2 11 global variable support (discussed further in the "Global Variables" section) is used to provide simple application-level switches to enable or disable arching functionality at run time, as shown in Figure 8. For static SQL, DB2 automatically prepares two access path strategies: one for use when archiving is enabled and another for use when it is not.

This approach is very flexible, providing automatic archiving and transparent access to archived data while also retaining the ability to disable that functionality via a simple SQL statement (or BIND option) when performance is critical and/or archiving functionality is not required.

Note that Version 3 of the IBM DB2 Analytics Accelerator product also offers some interesting options for handling archive data. For further details, see the "IBM DB2 Analytics Accelerator Enhancements" section.

Overall, the new transparent archive feature promises to significantly reduce the cost of designing, developing, and testing data archive processes for DB2 applications. While it will be of limited value for those applications that have already implemented such functionality manually, it could reduce developer/DBA effort by hundreds of person-hours for newly developed applications (or existing applications that did not originally implement an archiving strategy).

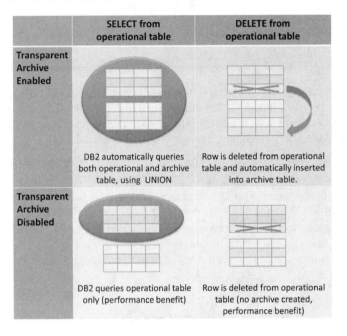

	SELECT from operational table	DELETE from operational table
Transparent Archive Enabled	DB2 automatically queries both operational and archive table, using UNION	Row is deleted from operational table and automatically inserted into archive table.
Transparent Archive Disabled	DB2 queries operational table only (performance benefit)	Row is deleted from operational table (no archive created, performance benefit)

Figure 8: Transparent archive behaviors

Solutions developed using this feature will also benefit from the ability to dynamically enable and disable access to archive tables at run time, ensuring that no performance overhead exists for processes that require access to only the current operational data.

Temporal Data Enhancements

Temporal data support, introduced in DB2 10, provided a unique set of facilities to allow data to be queried as at a specific point in the past, present, or future. With so many IT systems needing to accommodate a historical perspective and maintain audit logs of changes made to sensitive data, DB2's temporal support can save many hundreds of hours of design, coding, and testing that would otherwise be required to build this function manually for each application. However, the initial implementation had some restrictions, and, based on user feedback, IBM has enhanced DB2's temporal capabilities within the new release in a number of important areas.

Temporal special registers. Although the initial implementation of temporal query in DB2 10 allowed existing tables to be easily converted via ALTER TABLE, it was still necessary to alter the SQL in applications to include the necessary temporal clauses.

DB2 11 introduces two new special registers (CURRENT TEMPORAL SYSTEM_TIME and CURRENT TEMPORAL BUSINESS_TIME), which implicitly provide temporal context to SQL queries without having to change them. When the special registers are left to the default NULL value, SQL executes without temporal context as usual. However, when they are set to a past or future timestamp value, that value is used to implicitly supply a temporal context to all SQL subsequently executed within the session. Provided that the underlying tables are temporal, this enhancement makes it possible to quickly and easily make DB2 applications temporally aware without the need to make any code changes.

System temporal performance optimization. Access to DB2 10 system temporal tables required DB2 to UNION together the base and history tables for all queries. As the majority of the access to such tables tends to be querying current data, the additional access to the history table often posed an unnecessary overhead.

The new temporal special registers (described above) provide an opportunity to avoid this situation. Provided that a new option (SYSTIMESENSITIVE (YES)) is specified when BINDing the application, DB2 will prepare two separate access path strategies for queries against system temporal tables. As shown in Figure 9, DB2 will then use the relevant access strategy depending on whether the CURRENT TEMPORAL SYSTEM_TIME register is set. This approach provides the best of both worlds, with applications able to access historical data when required but avoid unnecessary performance overheads when it is not.

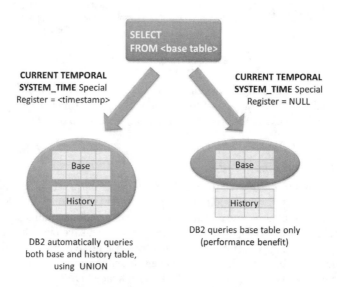

Figure 9: System temporal performance enhancement

Temporal view support. DB2 10 allowed temporal queries to be executed against DB2 tables but did not allow those queries to be executed against any views that referred to those tables. Because many customers use views heavily throughout their DB2 applications, this posed a significant restriction. DB2 11 removes this limitation, allowing non-temporal and temporal tables to be mixed freely within a view definition. Temporal queries can then be executed against the view, with the relevant AS OF predicates being applied to any temporal tables. Similarly, temporal UPDATE/DELETE logic is applied for any temporal tables updated via a view.

Together, DB2 11's temporal data enhancements significantly expand the practical use cases for DB2 temporal tables and will allow many more customers to take advantage of the substantial productivity and consistency benefits they have to offer.

Global Variables

One of IBM's stated objectives is to make it easier and more cost-effective to port applications from other databases to DB2. One of the major remaining barriers to this activity has been the fact that, unlike most other relational database management systems (RDBMSs), DB2 for z/OS did not offer support for global variables. These constructs make it possible for SQL statements within the same application context to share data without the need to use application logic or insert the data into temporary tables. Significant additional effort was required to rewrite applications designed for other RDBMSs that used global variables so they would work against DB2.

DB2 11 introduces support for global variables (Figure 10). You define global variables to DB2 via the new CREATE VARIABLE SQL statement, with metadata details being recorded in the DB2 catalog tables. As shown in the example, each application referring to a given global variable then has its own instance of it, which can be set and read independently of any other connection.

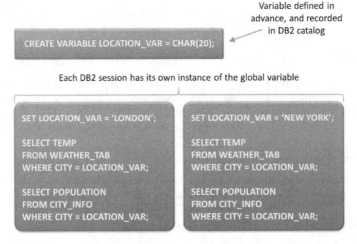

Figure 10: DB2 global variables

The availability of this feature makes DB2 much more compatible with other RDBMS implementations, letting applications be more easily and cost-effectively ported to DB2. It also opens up some valuable new possibilities for developers and DBAs to more extensively parameterize SQL scripts, with associated productivity benefits.

Variable Arrays

Many applications need to handle repeating groups of data with a variable number of elements. For example, a stored procedure to perform credit scoring may need to accept multiple customer account numbers as input to allow it to check several accounts at once. Variable arrays are a common means of addressing this kind of requirement, allowing an arbitrary number of elements sharing the same data type to be easily and elegantly addressed within an application.

Unfortunately, despite the growing popularity of SQL stored procedures for handling critical business logic, previous releases of DB2 did not provide support for array handling within the SQL PL language in which they are written. Therefore, such requirements had to be satisfied by various workarounds, such as defining a long list of differently named stored procedure parameters, using temporary tables to store data, or concatenating all of the data into a long string and then splitting it up again. All of these solutions have serious drawbacks in terms of efficiency, developer productivity, application maintainability, and code portability.

DB2 11 introduces formal support for variable arrays with SQL stored procedures. An array data type is formally declared to DB2 (via the new CREATE TYPE ... ARRAY SQL statement) and can then be used instead of a standard data type when defining a PL SQL variable or the input or output parameters of an SQL stored procedure.

Figure 11 shows the previously cited example of a credit scoring stored procedure that needs to accept multiple customer account numbers as input to allow it to check several accounts at once (up to 10 in this case). Before the availability of arrays, the SQL PL developer would have been forced to define separate I/O parameters for each element in the repeating groups as shown on the left. The same result is achieved far more elegantly and straightforwardly using arrays in the DB2 11 example on the right of the diagram.

For customers making extensive use of SQL stored procedures, the availability of variable arrays removes a major gap in the capabilities of the SQL PL programming language. As a result, SQL stored procedures can be written with less developer effort, will be easier to maintain, and will run more efficiently than their DB2 10 equivalents.

Java Stored Procedure Enhancements

Java® has long been considered a mainstream enterprise application development language, and many customers use it to write their DB2 stored procedures. As shown on the left in Figure 12, prior releases of DB2 used a 31-bit address space to execute these stored procedures, with each stored procedure running in its own Java Virtual Machine (JVM). This approach imposed a practical limit of two to five concurrent stored procedures within a single address space due to storage constraints and created a significant overhead due to the need to keep starting multiple JVMs.

DB2 11 addresses these limitations by supporting 64-bit multithreaded Workload Manager (WLM) stored procedure address spaces.[3] As shown on the right side of the figure, this allows a single JVM to support multiple stored procedures, with up to 25 per WLM address space observed in early IBM testing.

Figure 11: DB2 variable arrays

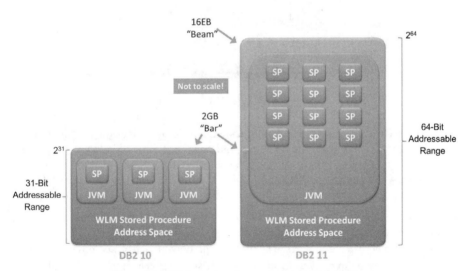

Figure 12: DB2 Java stored procedure enhancements

This enhancement greatly improves the scalability of Java stored procedures, reducing operating costs by lowering the CPU and storage overheads associated with many JVM instances.

pureXML Enhancements

DB2 9 introduced pureXML®—a major new feature that let XML documents be stored natively within DB2 and retrieved easily using the power of SQL and XPath. Some improvements were provided in DB2 10, and DB2 11 introduces an even more comprehensive package of performance and functionality enhancements.[4]

XQuery support. XPath and XQuery are two of the most common languages used for accessing XML documents. XPath provides a simple, extremely efficient way to navigate the internal structure of an XML document and extract specific information from it. XQuery can be considered a superset of XPath; as shown in Figure 13, it includes all the XPath syntax wrapped within a much more comprehensive, general-purpose query language that is able to undertake more complex operations, such as XML result set transformation and joins.

Figure 13: XPath and XQuery

The pureXML feature within DB2 for Linux, UNIX and Windows has supported both XPath and XQuery for some time, but until now DB2 for z/OS allowed developers to use only XPath. DB2 11 redresses the balance, allowing the full power of XQuery to be unleashed when querying XML data within DB2 for z/OS. This will improve developer productivity and DB2 family compatibility.

Performance enhancements to pureXML. The IBM development team has addressed a significant number of pureXML performance challenges within DB2 11. XML validation has been improved in several ways. The process can now be performed directly in binary format without having to convert to string XML first, LOAD is able to avoid revalidating XML if it has previously been validated, and DB2 is now able to revalidate only the changed parts of an XML document rather than the whole thing. Other performance enhancements include elimination of hotspots during XML INSERT and improvements to the XMLTABLE table function.

Figure 14 shows some of the CPU savings seen during internal IBM testing conducted during the Early Support Program (ESP).

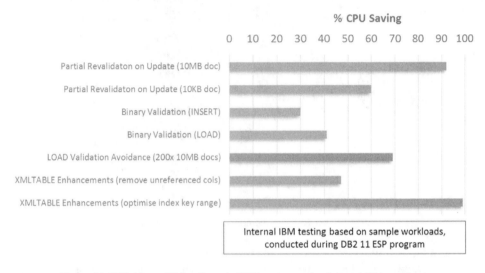

Figure 14: DB2 11 pureXML – Sample CPU savings using internal IBM workloads

The pureXML feature has rapidly matured to the extent that many DB2 customers have adopted it as their strategic XML repository. The availability of the powerful XQuery language and some very welcome performance enhancements further consolidate this position.

Optimizer and Query Performance Improvements

No new release would be complete without further enhancements to DB2's industry-leading optimizer, the key component that allows DB2 to pick the most efficient access path for a given query. Unless otherwise specified below, all of these capabilities are available immediately on entry to Conversion Mode for dynamic SQL, and at REBIND time for static SQL, with no changes being required to the application or SQL code.

The major items delivered as part of DB2 11 for z/OS include the following.

Hash join/sparse index enhancements. DB2 10 introduced hash join[5] support for access paths using an In Memory Data Cache (IMDC).[6] DB2 11 further optimizes memory usage by IMDCs to significantly improve query performance. At run time, DB2 will choose the most appropriate access strategy for each query based on the amount of memory currently available, as shown in Figure 15. Using this approach, DB2 can dynamically alter its behavior based on the specific workload executing at any given time, making best use of the memory available to provide optimum performance.

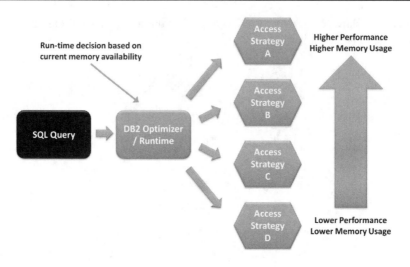

Figure 15: DB2 11 in-memory data cache optimization

IBM has also provided new trace data within DB2 11 to allow DB2 administrators to easily determine where performance could be improved by making additional memory available for IMDC operations.

These enhancements are expected to deliver measureable performance benefits "out of the box," but significant additional benefits are expected for those customers running suitable query workloads that are able to increase the memory available for IMDC operations[7] beyond DB2's default value of 20 MB.

Predicate indexability improvements. Using an index is generally the most efficient way to retrieve a small number of rows from a large table, but some predicates cannot be used to match indexes; these are known as non-indexable. It is often possible for a developer to rewrite a query so that the non-indexable predicates are replaced with indexable equivalents. This will permit the query to execute much more efficiently, but it requires the developer to have a deep understanding of DB2 query performance.

In some cases, DB2 is able to automatically rewrite queries to make predicates indexable, and DB2 11 adds a number of additional capabilities in this area. The following predicates have been specifically targeted:

- WHERE YEAR(DATE_COL) . . .
- WHERE DATE(TIMESTAMP_COL) . . .
- WHERE value BETWEEN C1 AND C2 . . .
- WHERE SUBSTR(C1,1,n) . . .

DB2 11 can also rewrite queries using OR predicates that involve NULLs to use IN-lists instead. This makes them eligible for a more efficient single matching index access path.

Figure 16 shows some examples of these new query rewrite capabilities.

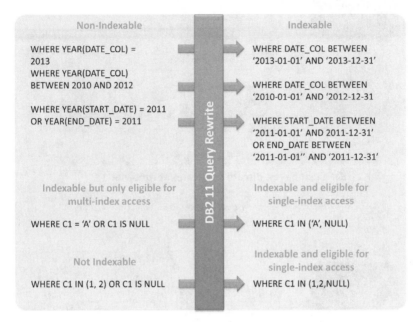

Figure 16: DB2 11 query rewrite examples

DB2 11 contains further enhancements to address SQL constructs typically seen in query generators and enterprise resource planning (ERP) applications. These include pruning "always true" predicates, extending the capabilities introduced in DB2 10 to prune "always false" predicates, allowing CASE predicates to be indexable and removing several other restrictions relating to conversion of correlated subqueries, and "pushing down" predicates into materialized views.

Duplicate removal. Many SQL operations require DB2 to remove duplicate entries in a result set, including SELECT DISTINCT, GROUP BY, and non-correlated subqueries. Eliminating duplicates can be done via sorting, but this approach can be expensive in performance terms, so several other techniques can also be used. DB2 11 introduces three significant enhancements in this area.

First, DB2 11 is able to more efficiently use an index to eliminate duplicates via a technique known as *index skipping*. Rather than read all the qualifying bottom-level index leaf pages and throw away duplicates at run time (as depicted in Figure 17), DB2 11 can use a combination of leaf and non-leaf pages to skip directly to the next distinct value, as shown in Figure 18.

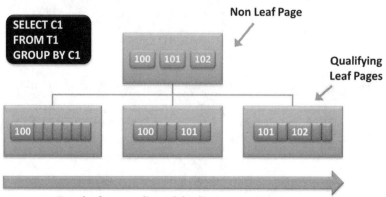

Scan leaf pages, discard duplicates at runtime

Figure 17: Pre-DB2 11 duplicate removal using index scan

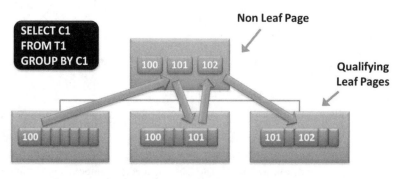

Use non-leaf page to determine location of next distinct value

Figure 18: DB2 11 Duplicate removal using index skipping

DB2 11 is also able to more efficiently process join queries that contain the GROUP BY or DISTINCT keywords, a common construct for ERP applications. This uses a process known as "early out" to abandon scanning the inner table after the first value has been returned, thereby avoiding the extra work needed to retrieve duplicate values and discard them later.

Finally, enhancements have been made to processing for correlated subqueries. DB2 11 can use another new early out optimization when the subquery uses the MAX or MIN function and can make better use of a result cache first introduced in DB2 for z/OS Version 2 for saving the 100 most recent correlated subquery execution results.

DPSIs and page range screening. Data-partitioned secondary indexes (DPSIs) were introduced in DB2 Version 8 as a means of providing many of the benefits of a secondary index while retaining good partition independence characteristics. While DPSIs can be very beneficial in some circumstances, they can also introduce performance compromises for some queries if they do not include predicates on the partitioning key. DB2 11 introduces some enhancements that significantly increase the "sweet spot" for DPSIs, allowing them to be more widely deployed.

First, page range screening for join predicates has been implemented. If a table is partitioned on one or more columns that are used in a join and indexes exist on other local or join columns, DB2 can apply page range screening from the join predicates and access only the qualified partitions for each table access. This behavior could significantly improve the performance of joins involving DPSIs.

The second enhancement involves improving the amount of parallelism available for queries involving DPSIs. If a table has been partitioned by a non-join column and has a DPSI on the join columns, DB2 can now choose to process each partition within a parallel child task. This can result in what was previously random I/O becoming sequential.

These enhancements are expected to provide a performance benefit for existing DPSI implementations, as well as significantly increase the sweet spot for DPSIs and enable them to be more widely deployed.

Optimizer RUNSTATS feedback. DB2's cost-based optimizer is highly dependent on both the quality and the quantity of table and index statistics available when it attempts to determine the optimum access path for a given query. While most DBAs have processes in place to ensure statistics are collected (via the DB2 RUNSTATS utility), most of these take the form of standard jobs using a common set of (or default) RUNSTATS options.

If the DB2 10 optimizer encounters poor or incomplete statistics, the DBA's first warning is typically when a poor access path is selected. He or she then has to determine the cause and (if poor statistics are to blame) re-run RUNSTATS with the necessary additional options. This process is time-intensive and error-prone, and it relies on deep DBA knowledge of the correct RUNSTATS options for a given situation. Figure 19 depicts this situation.

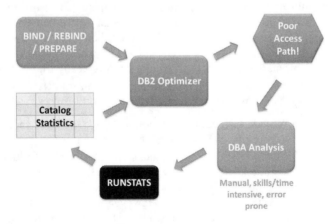

Figure 19: DB2 10 optimizer feedback issue

DB2 11 attempts to improve things by providing a means for the optimizer to signal when poor statistics are encountered (Figure 20). Two new tables[8] will be populated with the optimizer's recommendations on RUNSTATS options that would help it to select a better access path. Although this information unfortunately cannot be consumed directly by RUNSTATS, additional tooling can generate a suitable RUNSTATS job to address the issue. DB2 customers are free to write this themselves or use a vendor tool, such as IBM Optim™ Query Workload Tuner (which has been specifically enhanced to exploit this functionality).

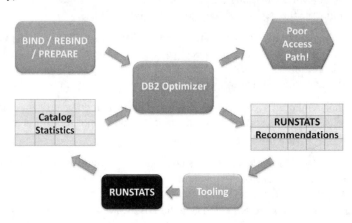

Figure 20: DB2 11 optimizer RUNSTATS feedback

With the necessary tooling in place, this enhancement can reduce the amount of DBA time spent addressing statistics-related access path issues and can help drive down operational costs by letting DB2 select more efficient access paths.

Extended optimization. During access path selection, the optimizer needs to determine how many rows will be filtered by each step in the access plan in order to determine the overall cost of the query. Most of the time, it is able make good estimates, either based on specific statistics or by using default "filter factors" based on the predicates in the SQL statement. However, there are some situations where the optimizer needs more help, especially with queries with pronounced data and/or execution skew[9] that use host variables or parameter markers. If this happens, the DBA typically tries to provide the optimizer with additional statistics (see the section on Optimizer RUNSTATS feedback above) or, in more extreme circumstances, may have to resort to access path hints.[10]

DB2 11 for z/OS provides an additional option by letting the DBA specify a "selectivity profile" for a specific SQL statement by inserting rows into a new table (DSN_PREDICATE_SELECTIVITY). This profile contains information about both the predicate filter factors and the execution frequency for a problematic query. A process similar to that used for access path hints can then be followed to allow the optimizer to use this information and select a better access strategy. However, unlike a hint, this doesn't "lock in" a specific access path and still leaves the optimizer free to select the best available access path based on the improved data and execution information supplied in the selectivity profile.

As with the RUNSTATS recommendations previously described, the DBA is free to either manually insert rows into the selectivity table or use external tooling to assist (IBM's Optim Query Workload Tuner will provide this functionality).

DB2 11's new extended optimization capabilities give DBAs a better alternative to access path hints where the optimizer is unable to determine the best access strategy. This has the potential to improve DBA productivity as well as drive down operational costs for problematic queries through more efficient access path selection.

Data Sharing Performance Enhancements

Data sharing was introduced way back in DB2 V4 and over the next few releases rapidly established itself as an unbeatable solution for customers requiring the highest levels of resilience and scalability. However, relatively few performance enhancements have been delivered since. Fortunately, DB2 data sharing performance has been selected as a focus area for DB2 11, and several significant enhancements are included in the new release.

Group buffer pool and castout enhancements. In a data sharing environment, the group buffer pools keep track of which data is being updated by which member and will also usually[11] be used to cache copies of changed data. If an application updates a page that another member might want to access, DB2 copies the changed page from the local to the group buffer pool so other members can see the new version (Figure 21).

There is no direct connection between the coupling facility and disk, so when DB2 needs to externalize the changed data, it is written to disk via a dedicated pool in the owning member—a process known as "castout."

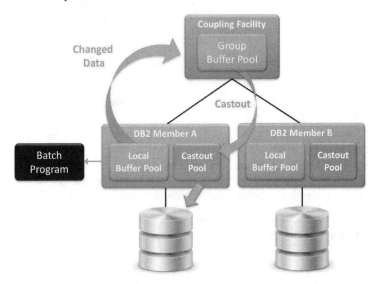

Figure 21: DB2 data sharing topology

In situations where there is heavy and sustained write activity to the group buffer pool (e.g., when running large batch or utility processes), a lot of changed data has to be written to the group buffer pool. In extreme circumstances, this can lead to storage shortages and can ultimately compromise data availability.

To help avoid this situation, DB2 11 introduces a new capability[12] known as *group buffer pool write-around* (Figure 22). This feature lets DB2 bypass the coupling facility and write changed pages directly to disk when the group buffer pool is under stress, significantly speeding the process of offloading changed pages. Once the amount of changed data in the group buffer pool has returned to a reasonable level, normal processing resumes.

In addition, castout processing itself has been improved to reduce the I/O elapsed time and optimize the communications between the coupling facility and the castout owners.

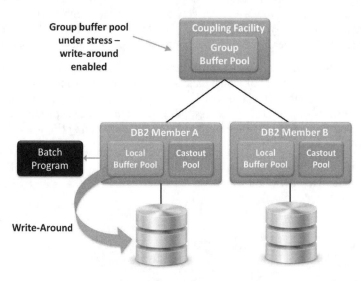

Figure 22: DB2 group buffer pool write-around

Other data sharing performance enhancements. Several other data sharing performance issues have been addressed in DB2 11, including enhancements to coupling facility DELETE_NAME requests to suppress unnecessary communications, a new option on light restart to include castout processing so that availability is improved, and various improvements to global locking and index split processing.

Together, DB2 11's data sharing performance enhancements promise to significantly improve data sharing performance while further increasing DB2's lead as the most scalable and available RDBMS in the industry.

Utility Enhancements

DB2 utilities perform housekeeping and recovery functions that are essential to keep applications available and performing efficiently. IBM's objective is to continue to drive down the CPU and elapsed time for utility operations while also reducing their availability impact and making them simpler to use. DB2 11 for z/OS includes some valuable enhancements in these areas.

REORG. A large number of enhancements have been made to the REORG utility. Improvements to online REORGs[13] have reduced the elapsed time of the SWITCH phase by up to 91 percent in IBM testing and provide more control over the timing, thereby improving availability. DB2 11 also introduces automated mapping tables,[14] improving DBA productivity and reducing the scope for human error.

Further new options allow the DBA to save CPU by choosing to reload data in the original order rather than sorting it and to reduce recovery CPU and elapsed time using partition-level inline image copies. Internal IBM testing showed a 28 percent reduction in elapsed time and a 49 percent reduction in CPU time when recovering a single partition of a 20-partition table space (Figure 23).

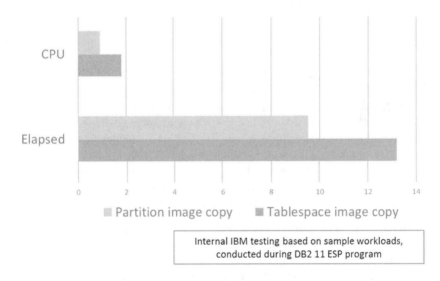

Figure 23: DB2 11 REORG – Partition-level inline copy

Other REORG enhancements include improvements to large object (LOB) processing, better support for rebalancing partitions following a partitioning key change (see the "Enhanced Dynamic Schema Change" section elsewhere in this paper), and updated defaults to reflect best practices.

Statistics. Collecting statistics is vital for good performance, but it can be expensive in CPU terms. The RUNSTATS utility has been enhanced to allow up to 80 percent of the CPU consumed when collecting distribution statistics to be offloaded to zIIP.

Improvements have also been made to inline statistics,[15] increasing the zIIP offload potential and allowing histogram and distributed statistics to be collected inline.

The "Optimizer and Query Performance Improvements" section describes an important new feature that lets the optimizer recommend specific RUNSTATS options to improve query efficiency.

Backup and recovery. Improvements have been made to the elapsed time for DB2 catalog/directory recovery, reducing application outage in the event of a serious DB2 problem. Other enhancements include the removal of restrictions for point-in-time recovery following dynamic schema change (described in the "Enhanced Dynamic Schema Change" section) and new options to allow more efficient system cloning when using RESTORE SYSTEM.

Other utility enhancements. Other utility-related enhancements include cross-loader support for XML data, increased zIIP offload for LOAD REPLACE processing, and significant elapsed time reductions due to parallel data conversion during load.

Collectively, these enhancements can significantly reduce operational costs by driving down CPU consumption while also improving application availability and DBA productivity.

Other Efficiency Enhancements

A number of other important performance and productivity enhancements are delivered in DB2 11, including the following.

Global Temporary Table enhancements. Declared Global Temporary Tables (DGTTs) are commonly used as an efficient way to hold intermediate results within complex processes such as stored procedures. DB2 11 allows logging to be disabled for DGTT processes, reducing CPU usage and log volumes (at the expense of some additional ROLLBACK considerations within the application). The CPU overheads for repeated COMMIT processing against DGTTs have also been reduced significantly by keeping prepared versions of the statement across COMMIT boundaries.

Pseudo-deleted index entry cleanup. Under most circumstances, deleting rows from a table does not cause the associated index entries to be physically deleted, but merely marked as deleted. These are known as *pseudo-deleted entries*, and large numbers of them can cause performance issues until they are actually deleted via a subsequent REORG INDEX. DB2 11 is able to use up to 128 asynchronous system tasks to clean up these pseudo-deleted index entries, using information it already maintains about the number of entries awaiting deletion within each index. IBM has provided comprehensive control options that allow this activity to be limited by number of tasks, index, time of day, and so on. All CPU for the asynchronous clean-up tasks is zIIP-eligible.

Figure 24 compares CPU degradation over time for a DB2 10 index and the equivalent situation in DB2 11 with the cleanup process enabled.

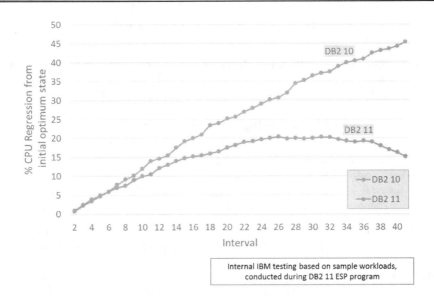

Figure 24: CPU benefit of pseudo-deleted index entry cleanup

Sort improvement. Several sort-related enhancements are included in DB2 11. These include increasing the amount of memory available for sorting, more aggressive use of in-memory sorting, and a reduction in latch contention. Because such a large proportion of SQL operations use sort in one form or another, these enhancements will benefit most DB2 workloads.

SELECT from directory pagesets. DB2 has always permitted users to issue SELECT statements against the metadata stored in the DB2 catalog, and this is a vital source of information for developers and DBAs. In contrast, the DB2 directory (which contains much of the same data but in an internal DB2 format optimized for performance) has remained firmly off limits. DB2 11 allows SQL SELECT access to five directory pagesets[16] for the first time, letting authorized users view DB2's internal data for diagnostic purposes.

Enhanced dynamic schema change. In addition to reducing planned outages and the possibility of human error, the improvements described under "Enhanced Dynamic Schema Change" can improve DBA productivity by significantly reducing the effort required to implement the relevant schema changes.

SQL support for analytic workloads. DB2 11 includes some SQL enhancements specifically aimed at supporting analytic workloads. These are described in the "SQL Aggregation Improvements" section.

Resilience

The System z platform is rightly famed as one of the most robust and secure computing platforms on the planet. However, business and regulatory requirements in this area continue to become more demanding, so this is an important and ongoing focus area for the DB2 development team.

This section groups together some key new features that make DB2 more resilient to the possible negative impacts of planned change, as well as increasing its ability to cope with ever-increasing workload volumes.

Extended Log Record Addressing: Current Issues

The DB2 recovery log records the changes made to DB2 objects and is critical for application and system restart/recovery. When DB2 was first released in 1983, it implemented a 6-byte log address (known as a log relative byte address, or log RBA), giving it the equivalent of 256 TB of total logging capacity. This amount was considered ample, allowing for many decades of logging at the volumes typical of the time.

Unfortunately, the relentless increase in transaction volumes, combined with a significant increase in log record size due to support for large objects (LOBs) and other new data types, has resulted in an explosion in DB2 logging volume. This has been exacerbated by recent trends to consolidate workloads into fewer DB2 data sharing members due to DB2 10's scalability improvements, resulting in yet greater transaction volumes within each DB2 system.

The net result is that many customers are approaching the end of the DB2 log range in some of their older or more active systems, as depicted in Figure 25. In some extreme cases with ultra-high logging volumes, this "log wrapping" is happening as often as every two months.

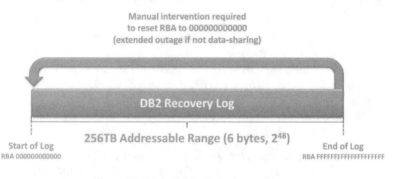

Figure 25: 6-byte DB2 relative byte address

In prior releases, resetting the log RBA was a painful process for non-data sharing customers, requiring extensive work and an extended outage of a day or more. Data sharing customers have a less disruptive option available, by "retiring" the DB2 system approaching the end of the log and adding a new one to replace it. However, even this option introduces additional cost and operational complexity, with changes required to operator automation, batch scheduling, and more.

A similar situation exists with the log record sequence number (LRSN) used by data sharing to provide a common log identifier across all members in a data sharing group.

The LRSN is also 6 bytes in length, but it is based on a clock value with a maximum that will be reached in 2042. While that may appear to be of no immediate concern, under certain circumstances[17] a "delta" or offset is added to the current clock value, and in extreme circumstances the offset can bring the actual LRSN value much closer to the 2042 high value. In Figure 26, Customer A has no LRSN delta and therefore has around 30 years of log capacity. However, Customer B has a very high LRSN delta of 25 years, leaving less than five years before running out of log capacity. Unfortunately, in releases prior to DB2 11, there is no way to circumvent this issue.

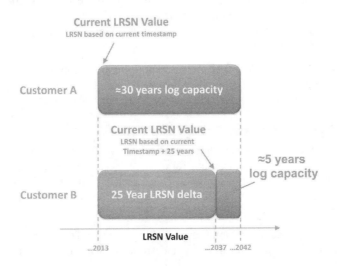

Figure 26: 6-byte log record sequence number

Extended Log Record Addressing: DB2 11 Enhancements

DB2 11 addresses the previously discussed issues by expanding both the log RBA and LRSN from 6 bytes to 10 bytes. For the log RBA, this enhancement provides 1 yottabyte (2^{80} bytes) of addressable range. To put that in context, the extreme DB2 customers currently wrapping the log every two days would be able to sustain 23.5 million years at the same logging rate before wrapping the expanded log (Figure 27).

Figure 27: 10-byte log record sequence number in DB2 11

For data sharing customers, 1 byte of the expanded LRSN value is used to extend the maximum clock value, with the remaining 3 bytes used to increase its accuracy. This provides in excess of 30,000 years of additional log capacity while also making the stored value 16 million times more precise (and thereby reducing performance issues associated with "LRSN spin").

Implementation of the expanded RBA/LRSN formats is optional but highly recommended as DB2 11 will use 10-byte values internally once in New Function Mode, and there will be a small performance penalty for converting these to the old format. Data sharing customers will be able to maintain full application availability by converting one member at a time, while non-data sharing customers will need to schedule a small outage (typically less than a minute).

The move to 10-byte log addresses represents a major investment in DB2's future and provides customers at or approaching the existing log limits with an elegant solution while also delivering some valuable data sharing performance benefits.

Enhanced Dynamic Schema Change

As applications evolve, the associated changes to DB2 objects such as tables and indexes remain one of the most common reasons for disruptive planned outages. Dynamic schema change allows DBAs to alter the definition of DB2 objects while maintaining access to the underlying data, with the change being fully materialized the next time the data is reorganized as part of routine housekeeping.

IBM began focusing on dynamic schema change back in DB2 Version 8 and has steadily expanded its capabilities in every release since. DB2 11 introduces the following additional enhancements:

Change partitioning limit keys. Partitioning a table can provide important scalability and manageability benefits, but it usually requires the DBA to specify a "limit key" for each partition so that DB2 knows which partition a given row belongs in.[18] Previously, changing the limit keys immediately made all of the affected data in the table unavailable until a REORG was executed to redistribute the data according to the new limit keys, making this a highly disruptive operation.

DB2 11 lets applications continue to access the table after partitioning limit keys have been changed. The DBA still needs to run a REORG for the change to actually be implemented, but this can be scheduled at a convenient time and with data availability being maintained throughout.

Drop column. DB2 has long supported the ability to add new columns to an existing table, but dropping columns that are no longer needed meant dropping and re-creating the entire table. Many DB2 applications therefore leave these unwanted columns in place, leading to wasted space, poorer performance, and maintainability challenges.

The new release extends the ALTER TABLE SQL statement to allow columns to be immediately dropped from an existing DB2 table with no application outage. As with the partitioning limit key change described above, this is a "deferred change," so although the column will no longer be returned if an application accesses the table, a subsequent REORG will be required to physically remove the column from the table data.

Recovery support for deferred schema changes. The deferred schema change capability introduced in DB2 10 and enhanced in DB2 11 (as discussed above) lets DBAs make schema changes at any time but defer the materialization of those changes until a REORG can be scheduled at a convenient time.

However, the DB2 10 implementation included a significant restriction relating to point-in-time recoveries. As Figure 28 illustrates, once the REORG was run to materialize the pending change (at T2 in the example), it was not possible to perform a recovery to a prior point in time. DB2 11 removes this restriction, allowing recovery to any valid prior point.

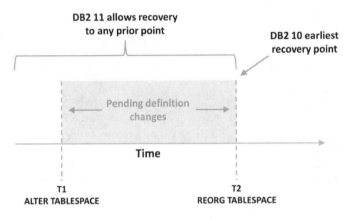

Figure 28: Recovery scenarios with deferred schema change

Together, DB2 11's dynamic schema change enhancements significantly improve data availability. They also reduce the possibility of human error and improve DBA productivity as a single SQL statement can replace complex scripts to drop and re-create database objects.

BIND/REBIND Enhancements

The plan management features[19] introduced in DB2 9 and DB2 10 went a long way to addressing customer concerns about potential access path regression during BIND/REBIND activity. In particular, a new BIND option let customers ask DB2 to attempt to retain the existing access path by specifying APREUSE(ERROR). DB2 would then try to reuse the existing access path for all statements in a package, but if that wasn't possible for even one of the SQL statements in the package, none of them would be rebound. This situation, illustrated in the top half of Figure 29, required the DBA to manually resolve the situation in order to successfully rebind the offending package.

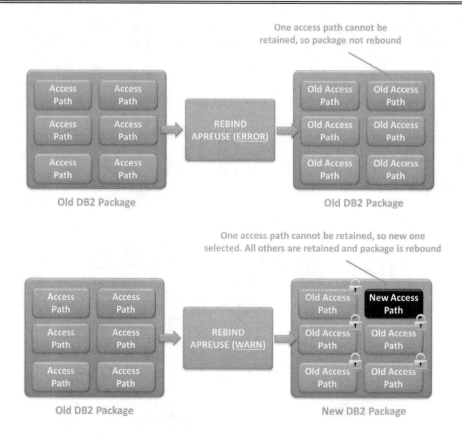

Figure 29: Retaining access paths with APREUSE(WARN)

DB2 11 introduces APREUSE(WARN), a new BIND option that provides more flexibility for the DBA. As shown in the bottom half of the figure, any access paths that cannot be retained will go through normal optimization to select a new one, while the access path for the remaining SQL statements will be retained.

This enhancement greatly improves the usability of APREUSE, especially for large-scale rebind activity such as that performed when upgrading to a new version of DB2. A greater proportion of packages can be successfully bound while retaining most of the existing access paths, leaving the DBA to review any new access paths as time allows.

Security Enhancements

DB2 received a comprehensive overhaul of its security features within the DB2 10 for z/OS release. DB2 11 adds some important new functionality.

RACF exit enhancements. IBM offers two options for managing access to DB2 data: internal DB2 security and external security managed by a product such as REsource Access Control Facility (RACF®). Many customers choose external security because this option lets RACF administrators handle access to DB2 objects using many of the same concepts, tools, and procedures as for any other type of resource. However, the exit responsible for communications between RACF and DB2 had some significant limitations.

First, the RACF exit did not honor use of the OWNER keyword[20] when plans/packages were bound or rebound and would instead use the authorization ID of the invoker of the BIND. Many sites rely on the use of OWNER within their DB2 security design, making use of external RACF security difficult or impossible. Similar restrictions also existed with the use of dynamic SQL if DYNAMICRULES(BIND) was specified.

Second, some situations could occur where access to a DB2 resource had been revoked in RACF, but DB2 would continue to temporarily allow access. In the example in Figure 30, USER1 is still able to access TAB1 after the RACF administrator has removed her access, because DB2 uses the internal DB2 authorization cache, which is not updated in line with the RACF database. Although techniques existed to force DB2 to refresh its internal authorization cache, they required manual intervention and could easily be overlooked.

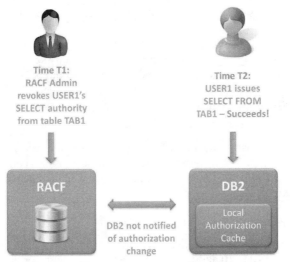

Figure 30: Example of RACF/DB2 authority caching issue

Both of these issues are resolved by the RACF exit changes delivered within DB2 11. A new installation parameter instructs DB2 to properly use the package owner for static and dynamic SQL authorization checks, ensuring that external RACF security behaves in a similar way to internal DB2 authorization management. Another new parameter enables a refresh function for DB2's internal authorization cache. As Figure 31 shows, this ensures that DB2's internal cache stays in step with changes made to RACF, thereby avoiding the potential exposure.

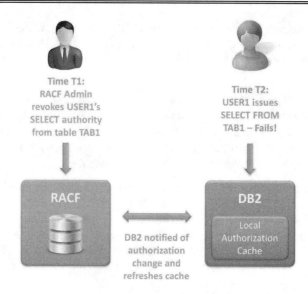

Figure 31: DB2 11 RACF/DB2 authority cache refresh

Column masking. The masking feature introduced in DB2 10 provided a powerful means of fully or partially concealing sensitive information by specifying a set of rules under which either the full value or a masked equivalent would be returned. (Typically this would be done according to the type of user making the request.) DB2 11 removes some of the restrictions previously imposed on the use of the SQL GROUP BY and DISTINCT clauses when querying a masked table.

Although less extensive than the security extensions delivered in the previous release, the DB2 11 enhancements resolve some significant issues and will allow more customers to take advantage of important features such as external authorization checking and column masking.

Other Resilience Enhancements

Managing persistent threads. The high-performance database access threads (DBAT) feature introduced in DB2 10 delivered significant CPU savings for many customers by letting DBATs retain DB2 resources across a COMMIT point and thereby allow a similar type of thread reuse to that enjoyed by CICS® users for many years. However, this feature also introduced some challenges in performing routine BIND and DDL activities, which could struggle to obtain the necessary locks.

DB2 11 includes some additional enhancements to allow it to selectively free accumulated resources for high-performance DBATs, making it easier for BIND and DDL activity to "break in" and complete successfully. This, in turn, allows high-performance DBATs to be more widely deployed, with associated benefits in performance and operational cost reduction.

Autonomics improvements. IBM has a stated objective of increasing DB2's ability to manage itself via new autonomic capabilities. DB2 11 includes new facilities to automatically clean up pseudo-deleted index entries (described in the "Other Efficiency Enhancements" section), and some improved techniques for reserving free space for SQL UPDATE operations to complete on the optimal page. In addition to improving DBA productivity, these autonomic facilities increase the robustness and availability of DB2 applications.

Scalability enhancements. Several enhancements have been made to remove DB2 scalability limitations. These include doubling the maximum number of open datasets that each DB2 system can access and increasing the maximum size of several internal objects to improve virtual storage usage.

Business Analytics

Traditionally, DB2 for z/OS was considered primarily an OLTP data server, with the DB2 for Linux, UNIX and Windows variant (or other vendors' databases) being a more common choice for analytics and data warehousing duties. This approach is often dictated by cost concerns or historical inertia, but the superior resilience and scalability of the IBM System z platform, combined with the increasing popularity of real-time warehousing, is leading many customers to re-examine this decision.

In a recent IBM survey,[21] 72 percent of the respondents indicated that they would be using transactional data from enterprise applications as input to their big data analysis programs. Given that both volume and velocity are highly significant in managing big data/analytics workloads, it makes sense for organizations to consider performing the analysis on the platform upon which that the source data resides.

DB2 9 and DB2 10 delivered some significant new functionality to support business analytics workloads, and DB2 11 further expands its capabilities in this area. However, some equally important developments are occurring within the supporting System z tools and infrastructure, and we will examine those as well in this section.

SQL Aggregation Improvements

Analytics workloads commonly require complex aggregation operations to be performed in order to summarize large amounts of data. DB2 has long supported simple aggregation via the SQL GROUP BY clause (as shown in the example in Figure 32). This capability satisfies many basic requirements, but more sophisticated business BI/analysis tools typically had to retrieve all of the detail/fact data from DB2 so they could perform more complex aggregation themselves.

DB2 11 extends the basic GROUP BY aggregation with three additional capabilities. First, the GROUPING SETS clause effectively allows multiple GROUP BY queries to be executed within a single SQL statement, as shown in Figure 33.

The example shows three separate aggregations (for week number, day of week, and sales person) being executed within a single SQL statement.

SALES_DATE	SALES_PERSON	SALE_VALUE	...
01/07/2013	John	123.50	
04/07/2013	Mary	43.75	
10/07/2013	John	4453.00	
10/07/2013	John	43.54	
11/07/2013	Mary	765.12	
12/07/2013	Mark	12.47	

SELECT WEEK(SALES_DATE) AS WEEK,
       SUM(SALE_VALUE) AS SALES
FROM SALES_DATA
GROUP BY WEEK(SALES_DATE)

WEEK	SALES	
27	167.25	WEEK(SALES_DATE)
28	5274.13	

Figure 32: GROUP BY example

SELECT WEEK(SALES_DATE) AS WEEK,
       SUM(SALE_VALUE) AS SALES
FROM SALES_DATA
GROUP BY WEEK(SALES_DATE)

WEEK	SALES	
27	167.25	WEEK(SALES_DATE)
28	5274.13	

WEEK	DAY	SALES_PERSON	SALES	
NULL	NULL	John	4620.04	
NULL	NULL	Mark	12.47	SALES_PERSON
NULL	NULL	Mary	808.87	
NULL	1	NULL	123.50	
NULL	3	NULL	4496.54	
NULL	4	NULL	808.87	DAYOFWEEK(SALES_DATE)
NULL	5	NULL	12.47	
27	NULL	NULL	167.250	WEEK(SALES_DATE)
28	NULL	NULL	5274.13	

Figure 33: GROUPING SETS example

The second new capability introduced by DB2 11 allows nested groups with subtotals to be produced, using the ROLLUP function as shown in Figure 34. The same three aggregation attributes as in the previous example have been used, but this time they are nested within each other, with a subtotal provided at each level.

```
SELECT WEEK(SALES_DATE) AS WEEK,
       DAYOFWEEK(SALES_DATE) AS DAY,
       SALES_PERSON,
       SUM(SALE_VALUE) AS SALES
FROM SALES_DATA
GROUP BY ROLLUP (WEEK(SALES_DATE),
                 DAYOFWEEK(SALES_DATE),
                 SALES_PERSON)
```

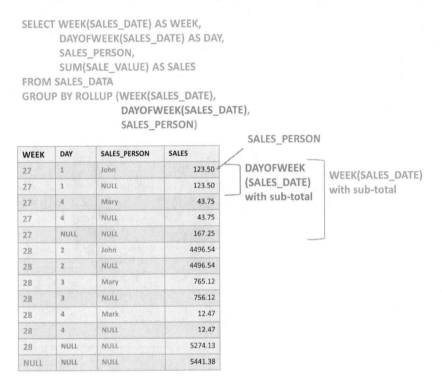

Figure 34: GROUP BY ROLLUP example

Finally, a GROUP BY CUBE function provides a similar roll-up functionality to the GROUP BY ROLLUP feature described above, but with the addition of cross-tabulation rows to create the equivalent of a data cube for slice-and-dice analysis.

These new functions significantly expand DB2's ability to natively aggregate large volumes of data, allowing BI/reporting tools to analyze DB2 for z/OS data with lower response times, and at less cost, than before.

IBM DB2 Analytics Accelerator Enhancements

Although IBM continues to expand DB2's native capabilities to more efficiently handle high-volume analytic workloads, it is very challenging for any general-purpose RDBMS to deliver the kind of query performance and efficiency that dedicated operational analytics appliances such at Netezza® can achieve without sacrificing OLTP performance. In recognition of this, IBM offers the DB2 Analytics Accelerator: a unique blend of

System z and highly optimized Netezza technology for efficiently handling complex, performance-critical, operational analytic workloads.

As shown in Figure 35, in an IBM DB2 Analytics Accelerator implementation, no changes are required to applications; they continue to connect to DB2 to issue queries. The DB2 optimizer is responsible for deciding whether a given query should be offloaded; if so, it is passed to the locally connected accelerator host for execution. Upon completion of the IBM DB2 Analytics Accelerator query, the results are passed back to DB2, which then passes them back to the calling application as if they had been obtained locally. Depending on the query, it is not unusual for IBM DB2 Analytics Accelerator queries that require hours to execute natively on DB2 to be completed in seconds once offloaded to the accelerator.

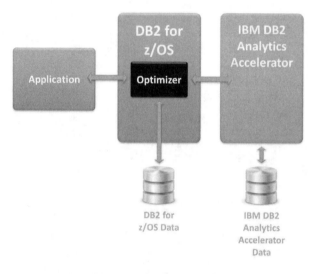

Figure 35: IBM DB2 Analytics Accelerator architecture

Version 3 of the IBM DB2 Analytics Accelerator technology, announced by IBM in October 2012, brings some significant enhancements that work in concert with DB2 10 and DB2 11 to expand the query workload capacity and capabilities.

Incremental update. As the IBM DB2 Analytics Accelerator stores its own local copy of the data to be queried, processes are required to keep the accelerator data in step with the operational copy held by DB2. Previous incarnations of IBM DB2 Analytics Accelerator only offered the ability to perform a full refresh of the data (at the table or partition level), which had obvious drawbacks for large tables with relatively low update frequency. IBM DB2 Analytics Accelerator V3 introduces incremental update capabilities, which allow updates to be trickle-fed to the accelerator data store and provide for near real-time reporting.

Multi-temperature data. The "Transparent Archiving" section of this document discusses one option for handling rarely referenced DB2 historical data, but IBM DB2

Analytics Accelerator V3 provides another by letting data be moved from DB2 to reside in the accelerator *only* as it ages. Also known as the High Performance Storage Server (HPSS), this provides a transparent means of moving rarely referenced data to a cheaper storage platform while still providing access when required.

Increased capacity. IBM DB2 Analytics Accelerator V3 extends the maximum effective capacity of an IBM DB2 Analytics Accelerator instance to a massive 1.3 PB.

Version 4 of the IBM DB2 Analytics Accelerator, which should be announced by the time this paper is published, is expected to include a number of additional enhancements.

Accelerator modeling. DB2 has long provided the ability for customers to determine the amount of CPU that could be saved by directing eligible workload to zIIP[22] engines. This enables customers to rapidly assess the ROI of potential future zIIP purchases. IBM DB2 Analytics Accelerator V4 provides a similar capability for accelerated queries, with new instrumentation to show the CPU time used for queries that would be eligible for offload to an accelerator (whether one is actually available or not).

More eligible queries. IBM DB2 Analytics Accelerator V4 significantly expands the number of queries eligible for offload. Static SQL queries are now eligible, and more DB2 data types and functions are supported.

Increased accelerator efficiency. Several enhancements have been made to improve the efficiency of the accelerator itself, including workload balancing across multiple accelerators, concurrent load/replication support, enhanced monitoring, and improved workload prioritization.

Enhanced HPSS solution. The HPSS capability introduced in IBM DB2 Analytics Accelerator V3 has been further enhanced with improvements to archiving functionality and the ability to more easily restore archived tables.

The combination of DB2 11 and the many new features in IBM DB2 Analytics Accelerator V3 and V4 significantly progresses IBM's objective to transition DB2 into a truly universal DBMS that provides the best characteristics for both OLTP and analytical workloads.

Hadoop and Big Data Support

Few IT professionals can have missed the big data phenomenon that has manifested itself in recent years. Despite the undeniable value of the highly structured operational data held within enterprise applications, a vast amount of less structured data is being generated by social media streams, telemetry, clickstreams, and many other sources. Being able to analyze these big data sources undoubtedly holds significant value for many organizations, but the sheer volume and velocity at which the data is produced makes it a very challenging task for traditional database systems. In response, a number of tools and techniques have emerged centered on the open source Hadoop framework, including IBM's InfoSphere® BigInsights™ technology.

While these technologies address many of the challenges inherent in analyzing big data, they also introduce new ones for organizations wanting to gain new insights by integrating the analysis of big data with core operational information.

As shown in Figure 36, DB2 11 delivers some highly significant new features to allow DB2 and Hadoop/BigInsights to work together and better leverage each platform's respective strengths. This capability lets data flow in both directions between DB2 and BigInsights, as follows.

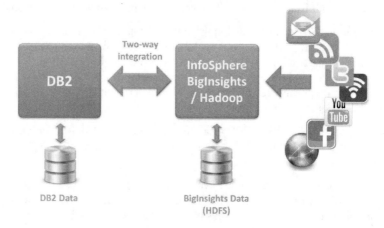

Figure 36: DB2 11/Big data integration

From BigInsights to DB2. DB2 11 provides new connectors and capabilities to allow it to easily and efficiently access BigInsights data. A query can be passed to BigInsights using a standard JSON-based query language called Jaql.[23] Once the query completes, BigInsights stores the results within its internal HDFS file system. A special new user-defined function (UDF) within DB2 11 then lets this data be read as if it were a DB2 table and even joined to other local DB2 tables if required. Figure 37 illustrates an example of this process.

From DB2 to BigInsights. In the opposite direction, DB2 11 data can be accessed from within a Jaql query running within BigInsights. This capability uses a Jaql JDBC module within BigInsights to allow Jaql queries to access DB2 (or any other Java-enabled DBMS), as in the example in Figure 38. DB2 sees this request as just another incoming JDBC/DRDA® remote connection, and returns the DB2 data to BigInsights, where it will be processed in the same way as if it had accessed native HDFS data.

This capability works well for low-volume queries that need access to current data, but some applications require a local copy of the DB2 data to be held within BigInsights/Hadoop for performance reasons. A tool known as Sqoop ("SQL-to-Hadoop") can be used for this purpose. Sqoop allows bulk data transfers between DB2 and BigInsights and can load the extracted data into a local HDFS cache.

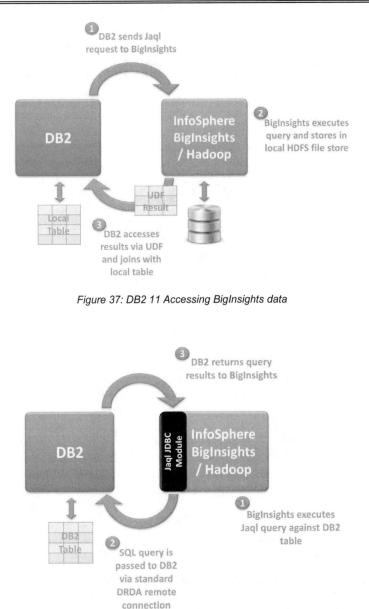

Figure 37: DB2 11 Accessing BigInsights data

Figure 38: BigInsights accessing DB2 11 data

The new integration capabilities delivered within DB2 11 allow organizations to more easily and efficiently combine the results of big data analysis with up-to-date operational data from DB2 OLTP databases, significantly increasing the practical value of any insights obtained.

QMF 11

IBM's Query Management Facility™ (QMF™) tool is as old as DB2 itself and provides a solid platform for executing many customer's reporting and analytics queries. QMF 11 will be released at the same time as DB2 11 for z/OS. It provides many new or enhanced facilities, including:

- QMF Version 11 Enterprise Edition includes a new product, QMF Analytics for TSO, which provides statistical analysis, forecasting functions, and additional chart types from an easy-to-use, menu-driven interface.

- Enhancements to QMF for TSO and CICS, including:

  o Big data integration, using the capabilities described in the "Hadoop and Big Data Support" section

  o Support for analytical queries using the SQL enhancements and IBM DB2 Analytics Accelerator enhancements described above

  o Better support for large data types such as LOBs and XML

  o Mobile device support

  o Broader support for temporal data

  o Improved report storage management

  o Customizable dashboards

  o Multiple database/platform support

  o Federated data support

  o Interoperability with other solutions such as SPSS®

- Enhancements to QMF High Performance Option, including DB2 COMMIT scope improvements and the ability for a single SELECT statement to be included in a query with multiple SQL statements

- Enhancements to DB2 QMF for Workstation and DB2 QMF for WebSphere®, including ad hoc reports, visual applications, and support for text analytics

Other Enhancements for Analytics Workloads

In addition to the specific analytic features discussed within this section, a number of other enhancements will be of direct benefit to BI/query workloads.

The significant CPU reductions provided by DB2 11 are directly applicable to analytics workloads and are expected to provide an immediate CPU/cost reduction of 10 to 40 percent for complex reporting queries.

Many of the optimizer enhancements will result in faster, more efficient performance for analytics query workloads (which are frequently complex and access large amounts of data) as well as traditional OLTP.

DB2's temporal functionality has already proven very valuable in many warehousing/analysis environments, which commonly have to support a historical perspective. The DB2 11 enhancements described elsewhere in this paper will add even more value.

DB2 11's transparent archiving capability could provide a useful alternative or extension to the use of temporal tables for managing historical warehouse data.

SQL PL enhancements for global variables and variable arrays should be of considerable interest within BI environments for the added flexibility they offer when constructing ETL processes.

Upgrading to DB2 11

This section outlines some of the high-level considerations around the timing and structure of the DB2 11 upgrade process.

DB2 Version Prerequisites

DB2 10 for z/OS broke with recent tradition by letting customers upgrade either from DB2 9 or from the earlier DB2 Version 8. IBM made it clear at the time that this was an extraordinary measure, specifically intended to help customers who had been unable to upgrade their Version 8 systems due to budget pressures caused by the global economic downturn.

True to its word, IBM is not offering a "skip migration" option for DB2 11. Customers must be running DB2 10 in New Function Mode in order to begin the upgrade process. This means that customers still running DB2 9 (or earlier) systems must complete an upgrade to DB2 10 before they can begin planning for a further upgrade to DB2 11. Figure 39 provides an overview of a possible upgrade decision process, based on the currently used DB2 release level.

IMPORTANT NOTE FOR DB2 9 CUSTOMERS:
IBM has announced that support for DB2 9 will be withdrawn in June 2014. As most DB2 upgrade projects require six to 18 months to complete, it is important for all remaining DB2 9 customers to begin planning to upgrade to DB2 10 as soon as possible.

Other Prerequisites

In addition to the requirement to be running DB2 10 in New Function Mode, a number of other conditions must be met in order to upgrade to DB2 11.

Hardware requirements. DB2 11 requires a System zEC12, z196, or z10® server supporting z/Architecture®. As outlined earlier, some DB2 11 features, such as 2 GB page frames, are supported only when running on a zEC12 server. DB2 11 is also expected to require increased real storage for a given workload compared to DB2 10.

System software requirements. DB2 11 requires z/OS V1.13 or later.[24] Some of the enhancements related to security also require z/OS Security Server (RACF) V1.13.

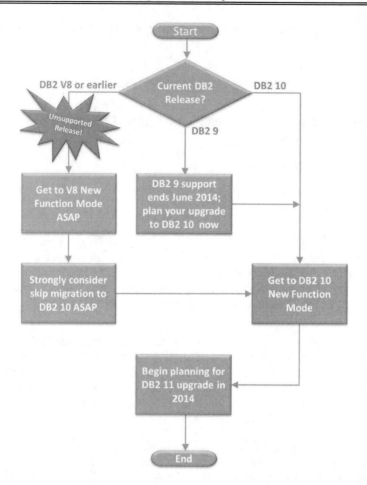

Figure 39: DB2 11 upgrade decision process

Application requirements. The new DB2 11 Application Compatibility feature removes the usual requirement for application code to be altered to address incompatible changes. Although the code will still have to be changed at some point in the future, this is no longer a prerequisite for upgrading to the new release.

DB2 11 does not support packages bound prior to DB2 9, so these will need to be rebound in preparation for the upgrade. However, the plan management features introduced in DB2 10 should significantly reduce the effort and risk associated with this activity (see the section on BIND/REBIND enhancements for a discussion of the DB2 10 and DB2 11 plan management features).

Upgrade Timing

Most DB2 customers will wait for at least 12 to 24 months after a new release becomes available before beginning their upgrade project, depending on their internal policies and the sophistication of their regression testing. As Figure 40 shows, adoption rates for DB2 10 were significantly higher than normal due to the significant business benefits that were quickly available within that release.

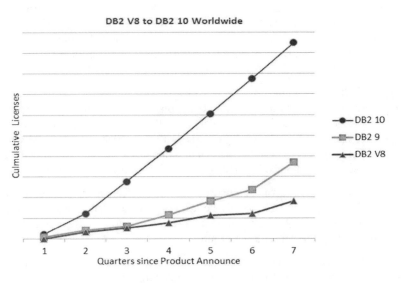

Figure 40: DB2 10 customer adoption

Recognizing the requirement for customers to be able to exploit enhancements and obtain business value as soon as possible, IBM placed additional emphasis on code quality throughout the DB2 11 Early Support Program with the objective of allowing a limited number of customers to upgrade their production systems before General Availability.

Each customer must carefully assess the business case for their specific environment in order to determine the timing for their DB2 11 upgrade project. However the emphasis on early production readiness, combined with the significant business benefits outlined here, is expected to once again result in higher-than-average customer adoption rates for DB2 11.

Upgrade Process and Impact

The process of upgrading a DB2 environment from Version 10 to Version 11 follows the same overall structure as previous releases. Each DB2 system is first moved into DB2 11 Conversion Mode (CM) before entering New Function Mode (NFM) via an intermediate step known as Enabling New Function Mode (ENFM). Most new releases require changes to be made to the DB2 catalog and directory (typically upon entry to the CM and ENFM phases), and this can cause some disruption to application workloads.[25]

Although the IBM recommendation is to schedule a full DB2 outage during the transition to CM and ENFM, business demands for true 24x7 availability are making it increasingly difficult for customers to do so. Therefore, recent releases have made it possible to reduce the operational impact by permitting some application access to continue during the upgrade.[26]

Further progress has been made in this area within DB2 11, especially with regard to the second set of catalog changes made on entry to the ENFM phase. This process is expected to require considerably less elapsed time than the DB2 10 equivalent and also to be less disruptive while it is executing. One test conducted by IBM against a large catalog from an ESP customer showed an 18X elapsed time improvement for the ENFM catalog changes compared with DB2 10.

Figure 41 shows the impact of the DB2 11 upgrade process for non-data sharing customers who want to minimize the operational disruption associated with the upgrade. A complete outage is still required to stop and start the DB2 subsystem and run the initial catalog update upon entry to Conversion Mode, but full availability can then be restored for the duration of the CM phase. Further catalog updates are required during the ENFM phase, but these can run alongside some normal application workload if required.[26]

Figure 42 shows the equivalent situation for data sharing environments. In this case, a complete DB2 outage can be avoided as one member of the data sharing group can be transitioned to Conversion Mode at a time, allowing applications to continue accessing the other members of the data sharing group.

Although the IBM recommendation remains to schedule a dedicated outage during the transition to CM and ENFM, the enhancements within DB2 11 further reduce the operational impact for customers choosing to conduct an online migration.

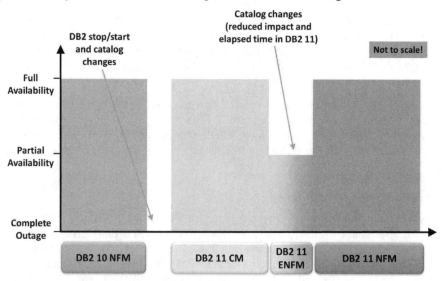

Figure 41: Application availability during DB2 11 upgrade (non-data sharing)

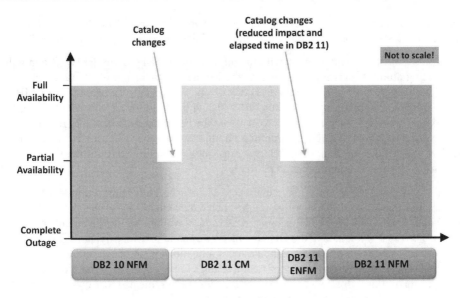

Figure 42: Application availability during DB2 11 upgrade (data sharing)

DB2 11 Customer Case Studies

This section is based on interviews with some of the organizations that participated in the DB2 11 Early Support Program. Based on their early experiences with the product, they outline the business benefits they expect by exploiting the features in the new release.

BMW Group

As one of the world's biggest and most successful car manufacturers, the BMW Group is at the forefront of both automotive and IT innovation. DB2 for z/OS is a critical component of many of the company's worldwide computer systems, from manufacturing to supplier management and customer ordering. In total, the German car company has more than 130 DB2 subsystems, belonging to over 40 data sharing groups and spread over eight z/OS LPARs.

BMW Group is no stranger to Early Support Programs. It participated in the ESP for DB2 for z/OS V2.1 way back in 1988, and more recently it was a key member of the DB2 10 for z/OS beta, which ran for most of 2010. "We participated in the DB2 10 ESP because at that time we were facing some real challenges with workload growth," said BMW Group's DB2 for z/OS Product Manager. "The CPU savings and virtual storage constraint relief offered by DB2 10 really helped us to cope."

Fast forward to mid-2013, and BMW Group is still enjoying healthy growth across its major markets, with all of the associated pressures that can bring to the supporting IT infrastructure. "Virtual storage isn't a big limitation for us anymore, but we expect the CPU savings in DB2 11 to provide the major business benefit for us," he added. "We are very early in our performance testing, but we have already seen CPU reductions of 8 to 13 percent on some workloads due to the more efficient decompression algorithms."

As part of the strategy to cope with the ongoing workload growth, BMW Group will also be upgrading its existing IBM system z10 EC servers to the latest generation zEC12 mainframes in the second half of 2013. BMW Group was an early adopter of the 1 MB large page frame support introduced by DB2 10, and the DB2 for z/OS Product Manager is looking forward to the opportunity to evaluate the benefits of the larger 2 GB page frames supported by DB2 11 when running on the new servers. "We use very large buffer pools within all of our production DB2 systems, so we're anticipating further CPU savings when we can begin using 2 GB frames."

BMW Group employs a highly centralized IT infrastructure, supporting all of its global business activities from within the Munich data center. That makes getting dedicated change slots difficult, so some of DB2 11's availability improvements are also going to be most welcome for the DB2 team. "We operate in a very dynamic 24x7 environment, and we often have to update our applications while they continue to operate. The ability to break into persistent threads and the enhanced dynamic schema change capabilities will allow us to react to business requirements more quickly and with less operational impact," said the Product Manager.

Another member of the BMW Group DB2 Team has been impressed with the stability of the new release: "We have encountered fewer install problems than we did at this stage with DB2 10, and our critical ISV tools are also stable, so overall we're very pleased with code quality. Support from the local IBM team, the IBM moderators, and the lab members has also been first class."

Perhaps the ultimate vote of confidence in the new release can be found in BMW Group's provisional plans for rolling out DB2 11 once the ESP program ends. "We are currently scheduled to begin upgrading our main DB2 systems in February 2014," said the team member, "with the objective of completing the rollout in plenty of time for our annual change freeze the following November." With DB2 11 likely to be less than 6 months old when the rollout begins, that's a powerful endorsement of the business benefits and product stability that BMW Group are expecting.

Stadtwerke Bielefeld GmbH

Bielefeld is a large city in North-Rhine Westphalia, the most populous state of Germany. As one of the largest municipal enterprises within the German energy market, Stadtwerke Bielefeld is responsible for the delivery of electricity, gas, district heating, and drinking water to the city's 328,000 citizens. The company's IT department runs IS-U, SAP's industry-specific solution for the utilities industry, and this depends upon DB2 for z/OS as its back-end data store.

Stadtwerke Bielefeld currently has around 60 active DB2 10 subsystems supporting SAP, spread across four LPARs of an IBM z196 enterprise server. After hearing about how DB2 11 could benefit the IS-U application at an SAP customer event, DB2 DBA Bernd Klawa recommended that Stadtwerke Bielefeld get involved in the Early Support Program. "The main reason to get involved in the ESP program is new functionality for the SAP Software," said Bernd. "The software layer for decompression is very valuable for SAP databases, since all Unicode table spaces are compressed."

Although the interview with Bernd was conducted before detailed performance metrics were available, he was able to share some encouraging initial results: "RECOVER of catalog and directory runs more than twice as fast as on DB2 10. The SAP IS-U unbilled revenue application (a batch workload) showed an elapsed time reduction of about 20 percent in Conversion Mode. After migration to DB2 11 New Function Mode, I saw automatic index pseudo delete cleanup, which should reduce the need to REORG after big batch runs."

Bernd also successfully tested the process of converting to DB2 11's new longer 10-byte log addresses. "The old 6-byte log address is not really an issue for our data center. However, the conversion will still be done when we move to DB2 11 for improved logging performance."

The experiences of Stadtwerke Bielefeld match those of many other ESP customers when it comes to the quality and stability of the new release. "I have been working with DB2 since Version 6, and I never saw such a robust release in such an early stage of development. The quality is very good," commented Bernd.

What about Stadtwerke Bielefeld's plans to upgrade their main DB2 systems to DB2 11 when the ESP program ends? Bernd is naturally keen to exploit the benefits within DB2 11 as soon as possible: "I expect to move to NFM in development and quality assurance systems as soon as DB2 11 is certified for usage by SAP."

JN Data

JN Data specializes in providing IT operations and engineering for large Danish financial institutions, including Jyske Bank, Nykredit, Bankdata, BEC, and SDC. DB2 for z/OS is a key component within this shared infrastructure, with around 100 DB2 data sharing members hosting development and production services for JN Data's customers.

The company recognizes the importance of staying abreast of the latest developments within critical infrastructure components such as DB2 so that it can continue to deliver the best service to its clients. JN Data was a prominent member of the DB2 10 Early Support Program and was keen to repeat the experience when the DB2 11 ESP was announced.

Although new development features such as transparent archiving are important, according to Systems Programmer Frank Petersen it's the operational enhancements that have the most immediate business value. "Features such as temporal tables and transparent archiving can save many hundreds of developer hours, but there is often quite a delay before a suitable application comes along to use them," he said. "Operational items such as the ability to interrupt persistent threads can be used almost immediately and will make a much bigger impact on us in the short term. I expect this will allow us to use some BIND parameters that should give some significant CPU savings and especially for highly used packages driven through persistent threads, which are used widely in our online systems."

What about other operational enhancements in DB2 11? "The move to 10-byte LRSN/RBA log addresses will also be important for us," said Frank. "We hit the RBA issue on one of our DB2 systems a while ago and had to take manual action to resolve it. We're expecting to encounter the same problem again within the next couple of years, so it's great to see a properly engineered solution from IBM."

Like their counterparts in many other organizations, JN Data's DB2 support staff never seem to have enough hours in the day. "We love autonomics. DB2 11 has some really nice features for reducing the burden on the DBA, such as the automatic cleanup of pseudo-deleted index entries." Sticking with the operational theme, Frank is also impressed with the improvements in the DB2 11 upgrade process, which make online upgrades more feasible. During its ESP testing, JN Data used IBM's Optim Query Capture Replay (OQCR) product to capture a few hours of workload on a real production system, then replayed that workload while attempting to upgrade one of its test systems to DB2 11. "It just worked, and the elapsed time for the catalog updates was much lower than before," said Frank. "Getting dedicated change slots for DB2 upgrades is a huge challenge with the number of systems we support. This will allow us to upgrade at a quiet time but without making the application unavailable. We'll be performing online upgrades for our main DB2 systems when we move to DB2 11."

Other operational pressures will prevent JN Data from beginning their DB2 11 upgrade project until 2014, but Frank is confident that DB2 will be ready when they are: "The ESP code mostly just worked from day one. The difference in code quality between DB2 11 and previous versions at this stage of the ESP is very noticeable."

Notes

1.   To benefit from DB2's improved ability to select the most efficient access path, a "rebind" will usually be required to allow DB2 to re-create the access path structures for an application. This does not require any changes to the application itself.

2.   Note that achieving these savings may also require the new log address format to be implemented; for further details, see the "Extended Log Record Addressing" section.

3.   64-bit multithreaded WLM stored procedure address space requires Java 64-bit JDK, Version 1.6.

4.   XQuery and some of the performance enhancements discussed in this section will also be retrofitted to DB2 10 for z/OS via the maintenance stream.

5.   Hash join is an alternative join method to the merge scan or nested loop technique and can be more efficient in certain instances.

6.   An In Memory Data Cache (IMDC) is an area of memory that holds intermediate work files when tables are joined. IMDCs were introduced in DB2 for z/OS Version 8 as a more cost-effective alternative to the sparse index technique used in prior versions of DB2 for z/OS. (DB2 can still use sparse indexes where insufficient memory is available to use an IMDC.)

7.   The memory available for IMDC operations is controlled by the DB2 DSNZPARM parameter MXDTCACH.

8.   The new tables are SYSIBM.SYSSTATFEEDBACK for recommendations generated during optimization of static/dynamic SQL during BIND, REBIND, or PREPARE, and DSN_STAT_FEEDBACK for recommendations generated during SQL EXPLAIN.

9.   Data skew describes a common situation in which data stored in a DB2 table is not uniformly distributed. For example, a table containing information about U.K. citizens may contain 60 million rows and 200 different cities for primary address. A uniform distribution should result in each city having 60,000,000 / 200 = 300,000 citizens associated with it, but the city of London will have over 8 million. Execution skew describes a similar concept, where some literal values are used in queries much more than others. Again, queries WHERE CITY='LONDON' are likely to be far more common than those WHERE CITY='WELLS'.

10.   An access path hint lets the DBA strongly suggest a specific access path to DB2, overriding the optimizer's usual cost-based analysis. This is generally considered a last resort and is usually discouraged, due to the additional effort required to create and subsequently maintain the hint.

11.   It is possible to configure group buffer pools to not cache changed data, but this unusual.

12.   This capability also requires a new coupling facility microcode level (CFLEVEL) to be installed. IBM plans to retrofit this function to DB2 10 for z/OS via the maintenance stream.

13.   Online REORGs let the majority of the work be done on a shadow copy of the data while full application access is maintained. The data is unavailable for only a short period at the end when access is switched to the shadow copy (known at the SWITCH phase).

14.   Online REORGs require a separate mapping table to be defined, which lets DB2 keep track of the relationship between the rows in the original table and those in the shadow copy. In releases prior to DB2 11, these must be manually defined by the DBA.

15.   Inline statistics are taken while another utility (e.g., REORG) is running. As that utility typically has to access all the data anyway, the overhead for simultaneously collecting statistics is much smaller than when running RUNSTATS separately.

16.   SYSIBM.DBDR, SYSIBM.SCTR, SYSIBM.SPTR, SYSIBM.SYSLGRNX, and SYSIBM.SYSUTIL.

17.   An LRSN delta may be set when enabling data sharing for a non-data sharing system. Higher delta values are typical when enabling data sharing on older DB2 systems, or repeatedly enabling and disabling data sharing.

18.   Note that DB2 10 introduced an alternative approach known as "partition by growth" that does not require a partitioning key to be defined. However, the traditional "partition by range" approach is more commonly used.

19.   This feature has several commonly used names, including "plan management," "package management," and "plan stability."

20.   On BIND, the OWNER keyword specifies the owner of the plan or package being bound, which must have access to execute all the static SQL inside the package being bound.

21.   2012 IBM Global Big Data Online Survey. Base: 60 IT professionals, multiple responses accepted.

22.   One of the ways in which IBM is reducing the overall cost of mainframe workloads is to offer customers the option to install additional "specialty processors" within their System z machines. These processors are capable of running only specific types of work, but in so doing they can reduce the load on the general-purpose CP processors and therefore the amount or chargeable CPU consumed. The zIIP is a specialty processor designed to offload specific types of data and transaction processing workloads, such as remote SQL statements, some DB2 utility processing, and network encryption.

23.   Jaql is a scripting language for enterprise data analysis based on the Hadoop MapReduce parallel programming framework. It was originally created by IBM and was donated to the open source community.

24. z/OS 1.13 has been available since July 2011, so this requirement should not be an issue for most customers.

25. The degree to which application access is disrupted depends on a number of factors, such as whether data sharing is used, the size of the DB2 catalog/directory, and the type of application workload that is active during the upgrade.

26. To minimize application impact, the catalog update process should be scheduled during a period of low DB2 system activity, when no changes are being made to the catalog by applications. This means that DDL and BIND/REBIND activity should not be allowed, but a small volume of normal application workload is acceptable.

27. FlashCopy is a function provided by IBM disk storage systems that allows near-instantaneous copies to be made of data. Other vendors provide similar functionality.

Acknowledgements

The author would like to thank the following people for their invaluable contributions to this paper:

- Mengchu Cai, DB2 for z/OS Development
- John Campbell, Distinguished Engineer, DB2 for z/OS Development
- Akiko Hoshikawa, STSM, DB2 for z/OS Performance
- Namik Hrle, Distinguished Engineer, DB2 for z/OS Development
- Terrie Jacopi, Program Director, DB2 for z/OS
- Jeff Josten, Distinguished Engineer, DB2 for z/OS Development
- Bernd Klawa, Stadtwerke Bielefeld GmbH
- Sheryl Larsen, World Wide DB2 for z/OS Evangelist
- Surekha Parekh, World-Wide Marketing Program Director for DB2 for z/OS
- Frank Petersen, DB2 Systems Programmer, JN Data
- Terry Purcell, TSM, DB2 for z/OS Development
- Jim Reed, Program Director, IBM Information Management
- Maryela Weihrauch, Distinguished Engineer, DB2 for z/OS Development
- Jay Yothers, DB2 for z/OS Development

Improved Query Performance in DB2 11 for z/OS

by Terry Purcell

The "out-of-the-box" performance improvement message in DB2® 10 for z/OS® resonated very well with customers and provided motivation for the DB2 for z/OS optimizer development team to look for opportunities to continue this theme in DB2 11 for z/OS (hereafter referred to as DB2 11).

Customers have rightly pointed out that "out-of-the-box" isn't really true for the optimizer, given that static SQL requires a REBIND to take advantage of new access paths and/or runtime optimizations. However, minimal intervention such as REBIND is certainly more desirable than requiring query rewrites or the creation of additional indexes to achieve performance gains. So while we aren't promising that all DBA intervention is eliminated, we certainly received the message loud and clear that "closer to out of the box" is preferred. For dynamic SQL, the first execution results in a new prepare, so dynamic SQL can actually achieve the optimizations out of the box. The vast majority of business intelligence and analytics workloads use dynamic SQL, and with the ad hoc nature of SQL requests in these environments, minimal effort to achieve performance improvements is certainly preferred.

One major goal for the optimizer development team was therefore to increase focus on query performance improvements in DB2 11 that required minimal action to exploit. Given that there is considerable diversity in customer workloads, the first question is how do you identify what would benefit the broadest set of customers?

Fortunately, there are operations that are common to a majority of workloads but are not necessarily part of the DB2 optimizer. DB2 11 for z/OS delivers performance enhancements to decompression of data rows and to sort (which I'll discuss briefly), as well as numerous internal code path optimizations that are not the focus here. But each of these improvements can enhance query performance generally.

The first task for optimizer development was to identify common query patterns. This job involved investigating customer workloads that DB2 development had obtained for performance testing, analyzing IBM and other enterprise resource planning (ERP) vendor-packaged applications and query generators, obtaining input from level 2 support on challenging query patterns, and studying lessons learned from customer proofs of concept (POCs) and migrations from other platforms. The results of this analysis were used to identify common patterns to target for DB2 11.

The following sections highlight the main query performance enhancements in DB2 11 for z/OS that require the least intervention to exploit, since these types of enhancements are of most interest for business intelligence and analytics workloads.

Predicate Indexability

Over the years, customers have been educated to understand that indexable predicates are the most efficient, while stage 2 predicates are least efficient. And, in traditional applications, developers were instructed by their DBAs to write their predicates so that matching index access was achievable for their queries. However, query generators, ERP applications, rapid development, and geographically dispersed end users can all result in limited ability for a DBA to control the quality of the SQL. So it is clear that there is a preference for DB2 to internally perform these rewrites or to optimize predicate performance.

DB2 11 rewrites some of the more common stage 2 local predicates, including the following, to an indexable form:

- YEAR(DATE_COL)

- DATE(TIMESTAMP_COL)

- value BETWEEN C1 AND C2

- SUBSTR(C1,1,10)   ← SUBSTR from position 1 only

DB2 9 for z/OS already delivered the ability to create an index on an expression; however, this feature required the developer or DBA to identify the candidate queries and create the targeted indexes. The DB2 11 predicate rewrites allow optimal performance without the need for this intervention. In some cases, an index on expression may result in better performance for the query, and, for this reason, if an index on expression exists, the predicate will not be rewritten to an indexable form in DB2 11. Index on expression carries other overhead, such as resolution of the expression during insert or update, and also applicability only to the targeted expression. Coupled with the need for the DBA or end user to identify the need for the index, the anticipation is that many of these use cases today do not already have an applicable index on expression.

CASE expressions are also enhanced to support indexability, as Figure 1 shows. It is increasingly common to see complex resolution of code values into their business value being included in a view or table expression for use within a query, rather than the use of a code table or dimension table for this purpose. When used in predicates, DB2 11 will now be able to use these predicates as indexable rather than stage 2 predicates as in prior releases.

Other patterns that have been optimized include OR and IN predicate combinations, which are common in ERP applications. In some cases, single matching index access is now possible where previously only multi-index access was available. And in other cases, multi-index access is available where matching index access was not possible before.

• For local predicate

```
• SELECT * FROM T1
   WHERE COL =     CASE (CAST(? AS INT))
                   WHEN 1 THEN 'A'
                   WHEN 2 THEN 'B'
                   ELSE 'C' END;
```

• For join predicate

- The CASE expression must be evaluated before the join.
- In this example, the join predicate is indexable if T1
  is accessed before T2.

```
• SELECT * FROM T1, T2
   WHERE T2.COL = CASE WHEN T1.COL = 'Y'
                  THEN T1.COL2
                  ELSE T1.COL3
                  END;
```

Figure 1: CASE expression indexability

In addition, query generators are known to add dummy WHERE clause predicates to simplify their generation framework—for example, WHERE 1=1. DB2 11 enhances these patterns by removing unnecessary "always true" and "always false" predicates in some instances. Customers who have historically used query tricks such as OR 0=1 or OR 0<>0 should note that these tricks will continue to be honored by DB2.

The final enhancement within this topic is related to predicate pushdown. Prior to DB2 11, only simple predicates were pushed inside materialized views and table expressions—for example, views containing DISTINCT or UNION. DB2 11 extends predicate pushdown to include OR predicates, stage 2 predicates, and outer join ON clause predicates. This change allows the filtering to be applied before materialization, benefiting those workloads that include views or table expressions containing DISTINCT or GROUP BY, and/or when these views/table expressions are used in outer joins.

The aforementioned predicate patterns cover a broad array of ERP applications as well as known customer pain points.

Duplicate Removal

Duplicate removal using either DISTINCT or GROUP BY is another common usage in query processing. DB2 11 for z/OS has been enhanced to improve performance of DISTINCT, GROUP BY, and also non-correlated subqueries when an index exists to provide order. In prior releases, DB2 has been able to avoid or minimize the sort overhead for duplicate removal by scanning a candidate index in sequence.

Figure 2 provides a simplified example of how DB2 11 can use the non-leaf key information to skip forward to find the next distinct key value. This technique is applicable for DISTINCT, GROUP BY, and non-correlated subqueries. Prior to DB2 11, DB2 would scan the leaf pages and remove duplicates internally before returning the data to the application. The main difference with DB2 11 is that DB2 can remove the duplicates earlier by simply skipping over them within the index, regardless of whether the distance between distinct entries is a short or large distance—although a greater performance benefit is gained when whole index leaf pages can be skipped over.

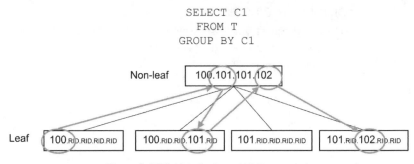

```
SELECT C1
  FROM T
GROUP BY C1
```

Figure 2: DB2 11 index key skipping example

Optimization of DISTINCT and other duplicate removal patterns extends to join queries in DB2 11 where the join is coded as an existence check. In such queries, any duplicates introduced from the join are not required for the final result. Figure 3 provides two examples of the targeted query patterns. In DB2 11, DB2 can "early-out" from the join to the inner table as soon as the first match is found rather than processing all matching rows. Prior to DB2 11, this type of early-out was available only to correlated EXISTS subqueries that were transformed to a join.

- In DB2 11, each inner table probe will stop after 1st match is found

```
SELECT DISTINCT T1.*
  FROM T1, T2
 WHERE T1.C1 = T2.C1
```

- Also applies to Non-Boolean term join conditions with "early-out" table

```
SELECT DISTINCT T1.*
  FROM T1, T2
 WHERE T1.C1 = 1
    OR T1.C1 = T2.C1
```

Figure 3: Early-out join examples

Correlated subqueries may also see a performance improvement in DB2 11 due to optimized usage of a subquery cache that has existed in DB2 since V2. Figure 4 provides a very simple example of a common query pattern used in temporal or time-based implementations whereby the most recent (or least recent) version is required by the query. DB2 11 optimizes this pattern by recognizing when order is provided and adjusting the cache size accordingly.

```
SELECT *
FROM POLICY P1
WHERE P1.POLICY_DATE =
(SELECT MAX(P2.POLICY_DATE)
 FROM POLICY P2
 WHERE P2.CUSTNO = P1.CUSTNO)
```

Figure 4: Correlated subquery pattern optimized in DB2 11 for z/OS

Hash Join and Sparse Index

Most database management systems provide a hash join method for efficient join performance when a suitable join index does not exist, or if a large percentage of the rows will be joined. In these cases, hash join can be more efficient than either nested loop join or merge scan join. Sparse index has existed since DB2 V4 for non-correlated subqueries; it was exploited from DB2 V7 for star join and was opened up to non-star join in DB2 9. DB2 10 added hash support, but only in cases where no index existed to support a join.

DB2 11 extends hash join support by allowing it to be chosen in more cases and by optimizing memory usage, including run-time validation of available system memory and appropriate fallback to sparse index when the result cannot be contained in memory.

While these enhancements are available after first REBIND for static SQL or next execution for dynamic SQL, it is important to note that the DB2 subsystem parameter MXDTCACH controls the exploitation of hash join. The MXDTCACH default is set conservatively at 20 MB; customers may consider increasing this value to gain further improvement. Although skill may be required for optimal setting of MXDTCACH, the accounting and statistics reports do provide a simple record of the number of sparse indexes where a workfile was built. This information, along with the number of synchronous reads in the sort workfile buffer pool, can be used as a guide to increase MXDTCACH or to reduce VPSEQ in the sort buffer pool.

Page Range Screening and Indexing for Partitioned Table Spaces

When local predicates exist on the partitioning columns, DB2 is able to limit the access to only the qualified partitions. DB2 11 extends this support to join predicates. This and other DB2 11 enhancements should increase the scenarios in which data-partitioned secondary indexes (DPSIs) can be used in place of non-partitioned secondary indexes (NPIs or NPSIs) to achieve improved utility performance without compromising query performance.

Given a partitioning scheme in which the table is partitioned by columns used in queries as join predicates, DB2 11 can use those predicates to filter out unnecessary partitions and probe only the qualified part(s). This enhancement is most effective when the index for the join is a DPSI and the partitioning column(s) either are excluded from the index or are not the leading index column(s). Prior to DB2 11, optimal join performance could be achieved for this partitioning scheme only if the index was created as an

NPI or if the index was partitioned but the partitioning column(s) was the leading index column(s) (meaning the index was a partitioning index, or PI, and not a DPSI).

Figure 5 illustrates a join between T1 and T2, where the inner table of the join (T2) uses a DPSI (on C1) and there exists a join predicate on the non-indexed YEAR column. In this example, each probe to the inner table can exploit the join predicate on the partitioning column to ensure that only the necessary partition is accessed for each inner table access. Prior to DB2 11, each inner table access would probe all partitions, with the YEAR join predicate being resolved after the data page was accessed. It is expected that customers were not accepting such poor performance previously, and thus the benefit of this enhancement is likely that a customer can convert to use a DPSI—which can ultimately benefit utility performance if this results in fewer NPIs on a table.

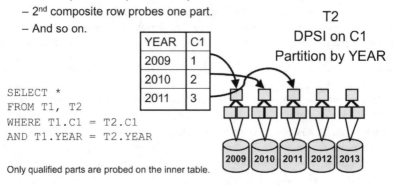

Figure 5: Page range screening from join

To further expand the use of DPSIs in DB2 11, there are additional enhancements for customers whose workloads already exploit DPSIs or who are considering moving more of their NPIs to DPSIs. A word of caution, however: While DB2 11 increases the sweet spot for DPSIs, there are still several scenarios where having one index b-tree structure (as with NPIs) provides considerably better query performance than one b-tree per partition.

When a query contains ORDER BY, GROUP BY, or DISTINCT and the query requires a subset of the table rows, an index is generally a more efficient way to provide that order rather than introducing a sort. For a partitioned table space, both a PI and an NPI can provide order that can match an ORDER BY, GROUP BY, or DISTINCT. However, a DPSI provides order only within a partition, not across the entire table space. DB2 can use one of two methods to allow a DPSI to provide order without requiring a sort:

1. **Have parallelism provide order.** With this method, each child task processes one partition, and the parent task merges the results to provide one ordered set.

2. **Use "DPSI merge" (also known as "DPSI return in order").** With this
    method, DB2 processes each partition serially, but a merge process returns the
    result in order across all partitions.

It is this second merge process that has been enhanced in DB2 11. First, index on
expression can now exploit the DPSI merge. Second, there are general performance
improvements to DPSI merge, such as improved index lookaside (and thus getpage
avoidance).

The next enhancement to DPSIs involves using parallelism for improved join performance when the partitioned table space is the inner table of a join. To benefit from this
enhancement, the partitioning scheme needs to be based on columns that are not included
as join predicates in a query. Figure 6 shows an example of this enhancement, which is
referred to as a *part-level* (i.e., partition-level) join. In this example, the table is partitioned by YEAR (note that each partition is numbered from 2009 to 2013), although the
query includes only join predicates on C1.

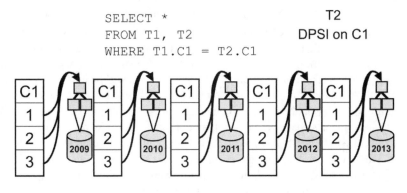

Figure 6: Part-level join

With the part-level join, each parallel child task processes only one partition, and the
composite (outer) table is shared or replicated to each child task. This allows each child
task to act as if it is simply a two-table join (involving one partition) rather than a join to
multiple partitions.

One of the traditional complaints with DPSI join performance has been that the join
would result in a large amount of random I/O since each partition was probed on the
inner table of the join. However, these two DB2 11 enhancements, page range screening
from join predicates and part-level join, should improve join performance for DPSIs and
potentially allow more workloads to convert NPIs to exploit DPSIs.

RUNSTATS Enhancements

RUNSTATS is crucial to the DB2 for z/OS optimizer to ensure that accurate information is
used for access path selection. And while running RUNSTATS is not a feature of DB2 that
we can claim is devoid of DBA or user intervention, many customers do have automated

or regular schedules for RUNSTATS collection. Thus, any enhancements that simplify integration with their schedule and/or improve the ability to recognize important statistics to collect are important enhancements.

DB2 10 delivered statistics profiles, which let customers combine the complexity of individualized statistics into a stored profile, which subsequent RUNSTATS executions could use to ensure consistent statistics collection. DB2 11 supports integrating these profiles into a LISTDEF, and when the USE PROFILE keyword is added to the LISTDEF, tables with a profile will collect their specialized statistics, while those without will continue to collect the basic statistics.

Next is simplified syntax in DB2 11 to clear out the statistics for a table and its associated index. The RUNSTATS keyword RESET ACCESSPATH will reset all statistics for the named objects back to −1s and clear out any specialized frequencies, cardinalities, or histograms from the catalog. Once you have a clean slate, you can then re-collect the desired statistics.

Finally, the major RUNSTATS enhancement is not actually an enhancement to RUNSTATS but guidance provided by the DB2 for z/OS optimizer about what statistics were missing as part of a BIND/REBIND, dynamic prepare, or explain. While determining the access path, the optimizer will externalize the fact that statistics that could be used by the optimizer were missing or conflicting. This information will be externalized to the catalog (from New Function Mode) and/or a new explain table (if that table exists). The DBA can use this information to determine what RUNSTATS to collect to potentially improve the optimizer's chance at choosing an optimal performing access path. Alternatively, IBM Optim™ Query Workload Tuner can interpret the information and provide the RUNSTATS input. Having the statistics recommendations externalized as part of general query processing is a significant step forward compared with the task of individually analyzing a query or having tooling collect a workload for analysis.

Additional Performance Improvements

The focus to this point has been on the targeted performance improvements in DB2 11, since readers need to understand some detail to determine the applicability to their workload. DB2 11 also provides performance improvements that apply generally to an entire workload, and these require less explanation.

In recent DB2 releases, sort performance has been a high priority, given that most workloads involve sorting and this is an area of resource contention because all tasks converge on the same sort buffer pool and datasets. DB2 11 extends in-memory sort capabilities for smaller sorts and temporary storage of intermediate results for some correlated table expressions and subqueries. There are also general code path length optimizations for sort and reduced workfile usage for the final sort. In simple terms, these changes mean reduced contention for workfile resources and improved performance for workloads that involve sorting.

Decompression performance is also improved, which obviously benefits workloads that issue queries against compressed table spaces. As with the sorting enhancement, nothing is needed to benefit from the enhancement.

Similarly, DB2 11 includes numerous internal DB2 optimizations, such as those to the DECFLOAT data type, which is used extensively in XML and also when workloads involve local or join predicates with mismatched data types, such as character to numeric. In such cases, DB2 uses DECFLOAT as an intermediate data type to cast for the conversion. DECFLOAT users should see considerable performance improvement in DB2 11.

Summary

DB2 11 for z/OS includes other query optimization enhancements that are not specifically outlined in this paper because they either require greater DBA involvement to exploit or are less focused on improving performance for business intelligence and analytics workloads.

What you should take away from reading this article, however, is that DB2 11 for z/OS is full of query performance enhancements that require minimal intervention to exploit—more so than in any recent DB2 release. We certainly listened to the feedback from the (almost) "out-of-the-box" message from DB2 10 for z/OS and expect similar feedback from the query performance focus of DB2 11 for z/OS.

IBM DB2 Utilities and Tools with DB2 11 for z/OS

by Haakon Roberts

IBM continues its industry-leading investment in DB2 utilities and tools. IBM has the broadest scope of solutions for IBM® DB2® for z/OS®. These solutions include business analytics and data warehousing, information governance, security, and industry-leading solutions in utilities and database management, performance, and backup and recovery.

Managing an enterprise database environment effectively and efficiently requires the right capabilities. Whether you want to tune application performance, simplify backup and recovery, track object changes, automate administrative tasks, or create clones for testing and development, you need management tools that streamline your ability to get the job done without adding excessive costs or complexity. Moreover, you need tools that can help you capitalize on the latest version of database software, DB2 11 for z/OS.

A number of business factors are driving the increased reliance on the capabilities of IBM's DB2 utilities and tools with DB2 11:

- **The need to provide global and nonstop availability of data.** This requires more than support for online utility processing. There is a need to support performance and administrative tasks that require no application outage.

- **The importance of reducing costs while retaining a competitive edge in the market.** IBM is the only vendor that recognizes the investments you have made in System z® and DB2 for z/OS with tools and utilities technology that capitalize on reducing the total cost of ownership. Being the first vendor to deliver zIIP support in tools and utilities, IBM is extending their support in DB2 11 to further reduce resource costs and CPU usage.

- **The rapid growth rate in both the size and complexity of enterprise DB2 environments.** This places an increasing burden on effective management of resources. There is a greater need to automate and simplify database adminis-tration and remove scalability constraints.

- **The desire to gain insight from data with the use of enhanced business analytics.** IBM introduced game-changing technology with the DB2 Analytics Accelerator for z/OS to help your business leverage its DB2 for z/OS operational data to perform business analytics in a cost-effective way. The DB2 engine as well as the IBM utilities and tools have introduced additional features that will enable you to get even more out of this new technology.

The IBM DB2 tools and utilities go beyond providing day 1 support for DB2 11 with closely aligned features developed to allow you to maximize your DB2 11 experience. The Utilities Suite has been enhanced with additional performance and availability features beyond DB2 11 support. The DB2 Utilities Solution Pack for z/OS, when used with the IBM DB2 Utilities Suite, lets you implement the latest features in the DB2 11 utilities with best practices.

One of the biggest changes in DB2 11 is the 10-byte relative byte address (RBA) and log record sequence number (LRSN) values to avoid hitting architectural limits. IBM DB2 tools and utilities such as the DB2 Log Analysis Tool, DB2 Recovery Expert, and DB2 Administration Tool, as well as the DB2 Utilities Suite, fully support the extended values and provide online conversion of page sets to the new extended page format.

Many of the DB2 11 features are made easier to use and manage with the IBM DB2 Administration Tool and IBM DB2 Object Comparison Tool. You'll be able to keep up with the latest features and modify existing tasks. For example, you can easily change a table from index partitioning to table partitioning in DB2 11 while keeping those objects online. The request is handled by the IBM DB2 tools, removing the complexity and details from the user while ensuring availability and protecting object integrity.

Many customers who used DB2 11 with IBM Tivoli® OMEGAMON® XE for DB2 Performance Expert were impressed with the ability to export spreadsheet data. This capability greatly accelerated and simplified the analysis of historical performance information. IBM clients using DB2 11 for z/OS also commented on the ability to clone their DB2 10 workload using the IBM DB2 Cloning tool and test on a DB2 11 system to eliminate any errors before that might occur during migration. This can greatly accelerate the time to market for a DB2 11 version upgrade.

The DB2 11 optimizer can enhance application performance by reporting any missing statistics. When used with the IBM DB2 Performance Solution Pack for z/OS and the IBM DB2 Automation Tool for z/OS, you can obtain the maximum ongoing value. You can automatically gather the missing statistical information and modify the relevant statistics profiles. This is a significant change in using statistics management to improve application performance by providing more meaningful information back to the optimizer to influence access path selection.

Providing timely and complete DB2 for z/OS version support in tools and utilities is a major goal for IBM. This support includes assisting customers at beta, General Availability (GA), and beyond. Each new release of DB2 delivers features and functions that are used to provide more value to businesses that use DB2. DB2 11 for z/OS support is no exception.

In summary, the IBM DB2 for z/OS utilities and tools portfolio is the most comprehensive in the market. These tools are unique in their ability to provide critical solutions to today's most complex business problems, spanning many functional areas to deliver the highest ROI from your software investment. DB2 for z/OS has a very robust history of providing efficiency, resiliency, and growth for your critical business applications. When DB2 is used with the IBM DB2 tools, you can accelerate your time to value for migration and use of new releases. You will be able to make use of new features in every DB2 for z/OS release with more confidence and less time and error. You'll be able to implement new versions of DB2 applications into production faster, with accelerated savings and increased performance.

About the Author

Haakon Roberts has over 25 years' experience working with DB2 on the mainframe platform spanning various aspects of systems programming, database administration, and software support. He is a Distinguished Engineer at the IBM Silicon Valley Laboratory in San Jose, California, and the chief technical architect and strategist for DB2 for z/OS Utilities and Tools. Haakon is a regular speaker on these and other topics.

How DB2 for z/OS Can Help Reduce Total Cost of Ownership

by Cristian Molaro

How can IBM® DB2® for z/OS® features reduce total cost of ownership (TCO)?

Total cost of ownership is a financial estimate that helps businesses determine the total cost of deploying a database over its life cycle, including software, hardware, and training. TCO analysis was popularized by the Gartner Group in 1987.

The goal of the following sections is to provide guidelines, orientation, and information about the elements that occur in the total cost of ownership of a DB2 for z/OS environment and to help readers explore ways to improve DB2 TCO in their existing environments. We start by setting the context in terms of today's business needs and how DB2 for z/OS can help. The following topics are then covered from a TCO saving point of view: synergy with System z®, CPU savings, better performance, storage savings, faster analytics, and improved scalability.

Business Needs and DB2 TCO

In 2011, the International DB2 Users Group (IDUG) conducted a worldwide study to understand the main IT concerns among database administrators, managers, and decision makers involved with DB2. Part of this study was a survey that gathered more than 1,100 answers from active IT professionals involved with the DB2 family of products on all platforms, but mostly on z/OS.

Figure 1 shows the distribution of the top answers to the survey question "What are the main concerns of your IT business?" The results reveal the two main concerns to be *Availability & Reliability* and *Reduce Cost*, followed by *Improve Performance* and then *Security*.

Availability & Reliability can be described as the need to assure business continuity. This aspect can be related to concerns regarding the guarantees of business survival. In today's highly competitive world, a relatively short IT outage can mean significant losses in both money and reputation. A serious outage can result in an organization being out of business permanently.

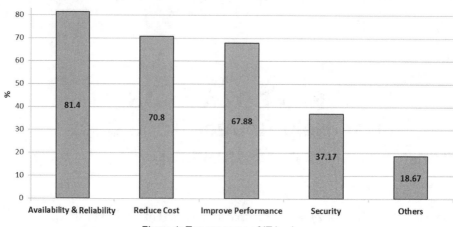

Figure 1: Top concerns of IT business

Reduce Cost also closely relates to organizational survival. The ability to provide the same or better service at a reduced total cost of ownership has been, is, and will continue to be one of the main objectives for any business evolving in today's competitive market. This point has been particularly true in recent years, during which the business continuity of many organizations had to be assured through cost reduction campaigns.

Improve Performance can be understood as the need to achieve faster response time and higher throughput to allow applications to cope with exigent and ever-growing business requirements. In many cases, good performance is a necessity for company survival and sustained growth. Improving performance relates closely to reducing costs, too.

Security has been a key DB2 industry concern in the past decade. Organizations have invested in seeking and applying technical solutions and policies to improve security. Security risks have tended to increase due to the inherent complexity and openness of Internet-exposed applications. DB2 security is becoming multi-layered, and security must be implemented at the physical, network, host, and data level. Security centralization is a trend today, and a common practice is to explore the potential of externalizing the otherwise internal DB2 security definitions.

That availability and reliability, cost reduction, performance improvement, and security are the main IT concerns is no surprise. These issues are the basis of the business continuity and business optimization definitions in the mature DB2 for z/OS industry.

How important the focus on each one of these concerns is varies with each organization. Each user differs, and so does its environment, context, and challenges. Nevertheless, reducing costs tends to be a common concern. Organizations face the challenges of aggressive business demands in terms of delivering results and better performance, but with IT budgets that tend to be under stress. IT organizations must deliver *more* business value with *fewer* resources. The ability to improve performance, increase productivity, and guarantee availability with a reduced total cost of ownership is, unarguably, a great asset.

DB2 for z/OS has been improving to help in this context. Recent releases have added functionality and features that can effectively help users improve the way they do business at a lower cost.

In this context, today's business needs are changing. We see our IT world evolving toward a near real-time, huge-amount-of-data, analytics environment. The mobile world, with its technical needs, is reaching many otherwise classic mainframe environments. A common consequence of the proliferation of mobile and other network-connected devices is an increase in online transaction processing (OLTP) workloads characterized by 24x7 availability requirements. These new workload demands are often associated with the generation of massive amounts of data and with fast analytics requirements. The market competition is highly competitive in many industries and services where DB2 is the core database. A strong need exists for fast analytics, online predictive analysis, data cleansing, and data integration, just to mention some of today's more discussed data-related topics.

DB2 for z/OS and System z provide the right platform to expand an already existing application environment to be able to cope with these new requirements. Thanks to DB2's synergy with the latest IBM zEnterprise® EC12 (zEC12) series of System z servers, the platform is able to deliver industry-leading levels of scalability, high availability, multi-tenancy, and ability to run mixed workloads.

DB2 11 for z/OS enhances DB2 analytics on System z with big data by providing connectors and the database capability that lets DB2 applications access data stored in the big data distributed file system Hadoop. The IBM DB2 Analytics Accelerator allows eligible DB2 for z/OS queries to be offloaded to an appliance to be executed fast, and sometimes quite fast.

Faster analytics, cost reduction through offloaded workloads, and straightforward deployment are accelerator characteristics that have the potential to make DB2 for z/OS and System z the best option for analytics.

DB2 and TCO

DB2 for z/OS celebrated its 30th announcement-date anniversary in 2013. When released, DB2 was intended to serve as a data warehouse database. With time and development, DB2 has evolved to become a state-of-the-art OLTP and data warehouse database engine. DB2 accelerators integrate with existing DB2 for z/OS servers to make DB2 a hybrid database. DB2 is able to deliver excellent transactional and analytic performance.

User requirements have a significant influence on the evolution of DB2 for z/OS and its features. As no exception, the strong industry need for cost reduction is guiding DB2 development toward a more cost-effective solution.

At the same time, the DB2 industry requires the usual level of reliability, high performance, and high availability that makes DB2 for z/OS and System z a business-critical, capable platform. New application development paradigms require features that enable DB2 to further support distributed access to DB2, to support new SQL, and to enable the new world of big data and analytics workloads. Helping users get more functionality makes DB2 a better but, ineluctably, more complex database.

The twin objectives of reducing costs and gaining functionality from DB2 pose an apparent conflict. Nevertheless, DB2 manages the challenges remarkably well. DB2 10 for z/OS provides a new, rich set of functionality together with CPU reductions "out of the box."

Often, the DB2 application environment hides savings opportunities that are readily accessible to DB2 users. The application of a non-used DB2 technique or a simple but forgotten best practice can help users achieve better results and reduce costs at the same time. In other cases, optimizations are the result of planning and applying DB2 functionality that requires application or system changes.

When looking for cost-saving opportunities, the main areas to investigate for potential benefits are:

- **Synergy with System z.** DB2 leverages and exploits the latest System z enhancements. This synergy may help to reduce TCO by providing better performance and more scalability to existing applications.

- **CPU savings.** CPU reductions can help to reduce TCO by lowering the software and licensing costs related to CPU utilization and by letting existing applications deliver more throughput as a consequence of reduced CPU utilization. CPU reductions can delay the need for a capacity upgrade and promote opportunities for server consolidation.

- **Better performance.** Performance enhancements unrelated to CPU improvements can help to increase application throughput, application availability, and the capacity to absorb peaks of application demand.

- **Storage savings.** In the context of large amounts of information, data compression and other techniques can dramatically reduce costs related to storing data.

- **Faster analytics.** Current business demands require complex analytics against large amounts of data. DB2's faster analytics capabilities help business to react quickly to changing conditions with reduced operating cost.

- **Improved scalability.** DB2 scalability enhancements allow better performance and throughput for existing applications. They may offer server consolidation opportunities, as well.

Reducing TCO Through Synergy with System z

Business demands and the requirements of fast-moving markets are putting data centers under stress. There is a need for smarter computing systems that innovate on efficiency, cost savings, and performance while lowering management costs and complexity.

The system design of the IBM zEnterprise System z addresses the complexity and efficiency requirements found in today's data centers. With its superscalar design, the zEC12—IBM's latest System z enterprise server—delivers a record level of capacity over prior System z servers. At its high-end configuration, the zEC12 is powered by 120 microprocessors running at 5.5 GHz and can execute more than 78,000 million of instructions per second (MIPS).

A Forrester study prepared for IBM, *The Total Economic Impact of IBM System z,* examined the total impact and possible return on investment that enterprises may realize by deploying IBM System z. In-depth interviews conducted with executives of five IBM System z customers revealed the following benefits experienced by the interviewed companies:

- **Reduction in server administration staff.** A centralized enterprise environment enabled improved staff efficiency, and cost-related reductions, compared with a distributed server environment.

- **Avoidance of costs related to maintaining a distributed platform infrastructure.** Fewer servers translated to reduced infrastructure costs, especially those related to space, power, and cooling.

- **Reduced storage cost.** System z's effective data-compression capabilities enabled reduced cost of storage. One organization reported saving up to 68 percent in storage when moving away from a distributed platform.

- **Cost saving from reduced downtime.** Companies were able to obtain a better level of availability for mission-critical applications, reducing the risk of financial penalties and image damage caused by downtime.

- **Better flexibility.** Organizations could respond more quickly to business needs and gain flexibility by exploiting the additional System z capacity.

- **Improved business credibility.** Some organizations reported that the implementation of System z improved their credibility with business partners.

DB2 Synergy with System z

DB2 for z/OS takes advantage of the latest improvements in the System z platform. With each new version, DB2 increases the synergy with System z hardware and software to provide better performance, resilience, and function for an overall improved value with a potential TCO reduction.

DB2 11 for z/OS leverages System z advances in large real memory support, faster processors, and better compression. It increases specialty engine eligibility workload, driving faster processing, improved performance, and CPU savings.

With zEC12, DB2 11 provides additional CPU reductions through the use of pageable large 1 MB real storage pages and Flash Express, and with the support of 2 GB real storage pages. DB2 for z/OS takes advantage of the following zEC12 features:

- **Faster CPU.** zEC12 provides faster CPU than previous System z processors, with a measured 1.25 percent faster speed than the previous z196 generation. The faster zEC12 processing capacity can provide these DB2 performance improvements over the z196 CPU:

  - 20 to 28 percent CPU reduction for OLTP workloads
  - 25 percent CPU reduction for query and utility workload
  - 1 to 15 percent less compression overhead with DB2 data

- **More system capacity.** zEC12 provides up to 50 percent more total capacity than the z196, making the zEC12 an excellent choice for fast-growing businesses and markets that need to fulfill ever-increasing processing capacity requirements.

- **zEC12 hardware features.** DB2 11 exploits hardware features of the zEC12 server, such as:

  - *Large frame area.* The large frame area is used for the 1 MB and 2 GB large real storage pages. Using large pages can improve performance for some applications by reducing the overhead of dynamic address translation, providing CPU savings.

  - *Flash memory and pageable 1 MB frames.* The zEC12 supports optional Flash Express memory cards. Access to flash memory is faster than access to disk but slower than access to main memory. Flash Express and z/OS 1.13 allow DB2 to allocate internal control blocks using 1 MB pageable storage, providing performance improvements.

  - *2 GB large pages.* A 2 GB page is a memory page that is 2,048 times larger than a 1 MB large page. DB2 exploitation of 2 GB pages improves performance by decreasing the number of translation lookaside buffer misses, by reducing the time spent converting virtual addresses into physical addresses, and by reducing the real storage used to maintain some internal structures.

IMPORTANT: With each new release, DB2 for z/OS leverages and exploits the new functions and capabilities introduced in the latest System z platform. DB2 11 for z/OS is no exception in providing synergy with the latest System z zEC12.

Reducing TCO Through CPU Savings

Reducing the CPU used by the DB2 subsystem or DB2 applications may result in a financial benefit. To estimate the potential financial impacts of a DB2 CPU reduction, you must combine and analyze information from different sources, such as your application CPU profile, the estimated DB2 savings for a given workload, and an understanding of TCO that relates to CPU utilization financial charges.

As an example, an estimation approach consists of the following steps:

1. Model the overall CPU utilization for a logical partition (LPAR), including DB2 and non-DB2 workloads.

2. Plot the CPU utilization and millions of service units (MSU) 4-hour rolling average.

3. Identify the MSU 4-hour rolling average peak and how it influences software charges.

4. Model the DB2-related CPU utilization (both system- and application-related).

5. Model the DB2 CPU savings.

6. Project the DB2 CPU savings on overall CPU savings.

7. Determine the DB2 CPU savings in the MSU 4-hour rolling average.

Figure 2 depicts this process. At a glance, a DB2 CPU reduction that results in a reduction of the monthly peak MSU 4-hour rolling average may result in an immediate financial benefit.

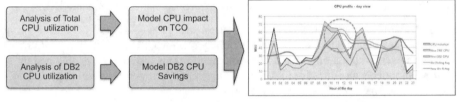

Figure 2: Estimating the financial impacts of a DB2 CPU reduction

A reduction in overall CPU utilization may impact licensing costs of non-IBM software, as well. Contact the independent software vendor (ISV) to obtain information about software charges and CPU utilization details.

How a given DB2 CPU reduction will impact the total cost of ownership is closely related to the System z software pricing model in use. Software pricing is a complex topic, and understanding it may require expert advice. The IBM webpage "IBM System z Software Pricing" at *www.ibm.com/systems/z/resources/swprice* provides an overview of IBM's mainframe software pricing, news about changes to IBM's mainframe software licensing/pricing, and downloadable tools related to System z software pricing.

The System z Software Pricing is the framework that defines the pricing and the licensing terms and conditions for IBM software that runs in a mainframe environment. An IBM Customer Agreement (ICA) contract provides the framework for the Monthly License Charge (MLC), which includes license fees and support costs that apply to IBM software products such as CICS®, DB2, IMS™, OS/390®, WebSphere® MQ, and z/OS. Software-related costs are measured by MLC pricing metrics such as:

- Advanced Workload License Charges (AWLC)
- Advanced Entry Workload License Charges (AWLC)

- Workload License Charges (WLC)
- Entry Workload License Charges (EWLC)
- Midrange Workload License Charges (MWLC)
- System z New Application License Charges (zNALC)
- zSeries Entry License Charges (zELC)
- Parallel Sysplex® License Charges (PSLC)

The MLC pricing metric is based on customer choice and/or the mainframe environment. You need to understand what the MLC pricing metric is to be able to model what the financial impact of a DB2 CPU reduction would be. Understanding how the type of MLC metric works will enable you to model the monthly license charges applicable to MLC products, such as z/OS, z/TPF, z/VSE z/VSE, middleware, compilers, and selected system management tools and utilities. Not all the IBM software running on your mainframe is necessarily an MLC product.

Organizations working with MLC metrics based on CPU utilization can benefit from immediate monthly license charges reductions as a consequence of reducing DB2 CPU.

Under sub-capacity workload license metrics, such as AWLC or WLC, the software charges are calculated based on the 4-hour rolling average CPU utilization per z/OS LPAR observed within a one-month reporting period. This information is obtained by the IBM-supplied Sub-Capacity Reporting Tool (SCRT) after processing of the related System Management Facilities (SMF) records.

Figure 3 is a representation of the CPU utilization per hour in a typical business day for a financial institution. The line in the figure illustrates the 4-hour rolling average for this LPAR.

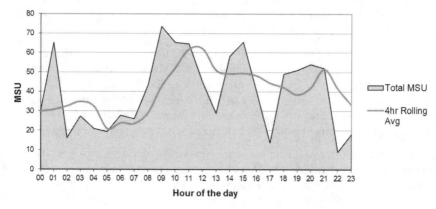

Figure 3: Hourly CPU utilization for a financial institution

The workload represented in the figure follows the common pattern of many other businesses, and we can identify two distinct workload patterns in the graph:

- During business hours, typically from 8 a.m. to 5 p.m., most of the workload is executed via transactions. This type of workload is commonly referred to as *online transaction processing, or OLTP*. An OLTP workload is typically characterized by many short, CPU-intensive transactions. This time period is also commonly referred to as *prime shift*.

- Outside of business hours, from 5 p.m. to 8 a.m. in this example, most housekeeping jobs are executed. These jobs or batches can be long-running processes designed to process large amounts of data. This time period is also commonly referred to as the *night shift* or *batch window*.

By combining the SMF and the DB2 accounting and statistics records, it is possible to model the percentage of total CPU utilization consumed by DB2-related processes.

The DB2 CPU used by applications can be obtained from the DB2 accounting records, and the DB2 CPU used by DB2 address spaces can be extracted from the DB2 statistics records. The total DB2 utilization is calculated as follows:

$$DB2_{CPU} \approx DB2_{CPU\_APPLICATIONS} + DB2_{CPU\_ADDRESS\_SPACES}$$

The non-DB2 CPU is calculated as

$$Non\_DB2_{CPU} \approx Total_{CPU} - DB2_{CPU}$$

For the same example, Figure 4 shows the DB2 and non-DB2 CPU distribution and the peak MSU 4-hour rolling average.

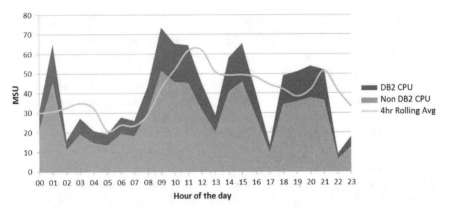

Figure 4: DB2 and non-DB2 CPU distribution and peak MSU 4-hour rolling average

Assuming a 20 percent reduction in DB2 CPU time, the new DB2 CPU can be modeled as follows:

$$New\_DB2_{CPU} \approx (DB2_{CPU\_APPLICATIONS} + DB2_{CPU\_ADDRESS\_SPACES}) * (1 - DB2_{SAVINGS})$$

As the CPU reduction pertains to DB2, the non-DB2 CPU utilization remains unaltered. As a result, the total CPU utilization can be recalculated as:

$$Total_{CPU} \approx Non\_DB2_{CPU} + New\_DB2_{CPU}$$

The new total CPU allows us to obtain a recalculated MSU 4 hour rolling average, as shown in Figure 5.

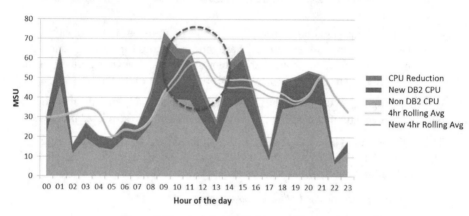

Figure 5: Recalculated MSU 4-hour rolling average

In this example, in which only 30 percent of the total CPU in the LPAR was DB2-related, a DB2 CPU reduction of 20 percent leads to a reduction of 8 percent in the peak MSU 4-hour rolling average. This reduction may be reflected in the monthly license charges.

The calculated percentage may or may not be linearly applicable to eligible software licenses; the unitary MSU price is grouped by cumulative monthly pricing levels as defined in the Advanced Workload License Charges Structure. At a glance, the more MSUs used, the less expensive they are. The focus must be the peak period. A CPU improvement, or a CPU regression, that does not affect the monthly MSU peak 4-hour rolling average may be, at least in this context, transparent from a financial point of view.

DB2 10 CPU Savings and Performance Improvements

When migrating from DB2 9, you start from DB2 9 New Function Mode (NFM). The first stage in DB2 10 is DB2 10 Conversion Mode (CM9); from here, you can fall back to DB2 9 if required. The next steps are DB2 V10 Enabling New Function Mode (ENFM9) and DB2 10 New Function Mode (NFM). DB2 10 also supports skip release migration, letting you migrate directly from DB2 8 NFM. Figure 6 illustrates these migration paths.

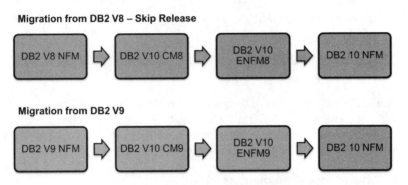

Figure 6: DB2 10 for z/OS migration paths

The maximum performance potential is available in DB2 10 NFM. However, because DB2 10 delivers many of its performance benefits in Conversion Mode, the first migration step is also interesting from a performance point of view. Some of the most relevant DB2 10 performance features grouped by migration step are listed in this section.

- DB2 10 Conversion Mode:
    o Improved performance of SQL at runtime
    o Faster single-row retrievals via open-fetch-close chaining
    o Parallel index update at insert
    o Query parallelism improvements
    o Workfile in-memory enhancements
    o Insert improvement for universal table spaces (UTS)
    o Index list prefetch
    o Memory changes exploiting more 64-bit storage, some after REBIND
    o Increased Distributed Data Facility (DDF) performance (high-performance database access threads, or Hiper-DBATs)
    o Buffer pool enhancements

- DB2 10 New Function Mode:
    o Efficient caching of dynamic SQL statements with literals
    o Faster fetch and insert
    o SQL Procedural Language (PL) performance improvements
    o MEMBER CLUSTER for universal table spaces (UTSs)
    o Utility enhancements

- DB2 10 New Function Mode features requiring changes:
  - ○ Hash access path
  - ○ Index include columns
  - ○ Inline large objects (LOBs)

A detailed description of these features is beyond the scope of this document. Functional details are available in the IBM Redbook *DB2 10 for z/OS Technical Overview* (SG24-7892). Performance considerations and observations are reported in the IBM Redbook *DB2 10 for z/OS Performance Topics* (SG24-7942).

DB2 10 Performance Expectations

Because each organization, each application, and each environment is unique, it is not practical to design a single standard methodology that can forecast how much resource utilization improvement, or savings, you can get from any new DB2 version. Most workloads may show up to 10 percent CPU reduction for static SQL after REBIND. You may observe an even greater improvement with workloads that had scalability issues in previous versions of DB2 or in distributed applications targeting DB2 for z/OS and exploiting DRDA and dynamic SQL.

Some workloads are particularly susceptible to showing substantial savings. For example, those exploiting native SQL PL procedures can see up to 20 percent CPU reduction. Query workloads will also show significant improvements as a result of many positive access path changes.

Figure 7 shows the results obtained by IBM under controlled and repeatable workload conditions.

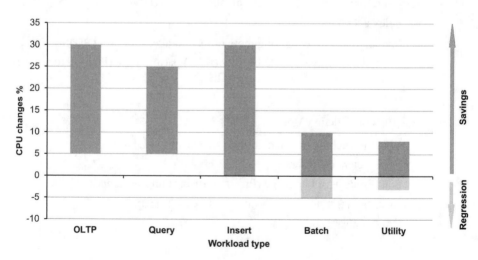

Figure 7: DB2 9 to DB2 10 migration and CPU changes – IBM benchmarks

These results are grouped by workload category. Positive changes, expressed as percentages, indicate CPU savings. Negative values indicate CPU regression. In most cases, the benchmarks were based on customer data, and these results were almost always confirmed by the customer running DB2 10.

The tests were done under controlled conditions and are repeatable, a requirement for quality statistical analysis. The benchmark results enforce the concept of variance in the expected savings: CPU improvement is workload-dependent, and your results will also vary.

DB2 11 CPU Savings and Performance Improvements

The migration to DB2 11 starts in DB2 10 NFM. There is no support for skip migration; you cannot migrate to DB2 11 from DB2 9 (Figure 8). In terms of performance enhancements, DB2 11 focuses on two areas: CPU and cost reduction and scalability.

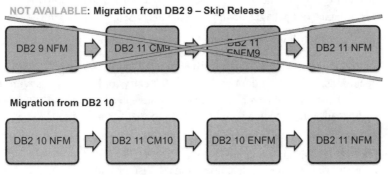

Figure 8: DB2 11 migration path

Many changes target areas that are commonly a source of performance concerns. For example, DB2 11 focuses on providing consistent performance to applications that change data, and it reduces the need for REORG utilities in some scenarios. DB2 11 has the ability to react to workload changes, requiring fewer efforts in performance tuning.

DB2 11 system performance changes that help to reduce CPU utilization include:

- Additional ad hoc machine code generation is provided for repeated operations such as SQL column processing (column proc) and RDS sort operations (sort proc).

- A new data decompression routine provides significant CPU reduction and speeds up expansion operations.

- DB2 log large RBA/LRSN support removes LRSN spin in data sharing environments. This change can provide significant CPU reduction in batch write operations.

- The DB2 output log buffer is moved to 64-bit common storage, reducing CPU by removing cross address space operation for logging. IBM reports significant CPU reduction due to this enhancement in update-intensive batch jobs.

- Data sharing availability and performance improvements, including:

  o Improved CASTOUT performance and faster CASTOUT

  o Conditional activation of group buffer pool (GBP) write-around makes pages be written directly to DASD

  o Coupling Facility DELETE NAME enhancement

  o Internal Resources Lock Manager (IRLM) enhancements

Two of the main DB2 performance changes that provide better scalability are:

- Internal DB2 processing units (zProcs) are moved above the 2 GB storage bar, providing further reduction of DBM1 virtual storage utilization below the bar. z/OS 1.13 made possible 64-bit code execution and code optimization for zProcs.

- Scalability improvement with a large number of partitions improves the performance of packages bound with the RELEASE(COMMIT) option.

DB2 11 application-level performance improvements include the following:

- When EXCLUDE NULL KEYS is specified in CREATE INDEX and ALTER INDEX operations, DB2 11 will not create an index entry for key columns with NULL. Benefits include reduced cost of index maintenance, potential FETCH performance improvement, and reduced index space utilization.

- The DECLARE GLOBAL TEMPORARY TABLES statement adds support for NOT LOGGED. This change can provide significant CPU and elapsed time reductions in intensive insert and update operations. It also provides significantly faster rollback.

- SORT improvements extend the scope of the in-memory sort operations in DB2 11. Changes can reduce workfile physical usage for large top-level sort, lowering CPU and elapsed time for sort operations.

Specialty engines provide a highly effective way to reduce CPU costs by offloading a part of CPU execution from a general-purpose processor to a special processor. DB2 11 continues the trend of increasing the zIIP value by expanding DB2 CPU zIIP eligibility for utility and system tasks workloads. (The value of zIIPs is discussed later.)

DB2 11 Performance Expectations

DB2 10 delivered strong DB2 CPU savings that drove great value for IBM users. DB2 11 follows up with even more CPU savings and improved performance. IBM's internal testing and Early Support Program results show that, depending on the specific workload, clients may achieve "out-of-the-box" DB2 CPU savings of up to 10 percent for complex OLTP workloads and up to 10 percent for update-intensive batch workloads. Complex reporting queries can see up to 25 percent CPU savings for uncompressed tables and up to 40 percent when running queries against compressed tables. These results are com-pared with running the same workloads on DB2 10. Additional CPU savings and performance improvements may be possible with application and/or system changes that take advantage of new DB2 11 enhancements such as log replication capture, data sharing using the extended log record format, and pureXML.

As with each DB2 release, some workloads are particularly susceptible to showing significant CPU savings in DB2 11. These workloads are often referred to as the performance "sweet spots."

In DB2 11, write-intensive batches are an excellent candidate to show CPU savings. For OLTP workloads, better performance improvements are expected for workloads involving write-intensive transactions. Transactions using RELEASE(COMMIT) and involving objects with many (more than 200) partitions are excellent candidates to obtain CPU benefits.

Distributed applications featuring workloads with heavy network traffic may show CPU benefits as a result of the synergy between DB2 11 and changes in z/OS Communications Server.

Performance sweet spots for query workload (e.g., data warehousing SQL) include those working with compressed tables and those exploiting SORT intensively. SQL access path enhancements can provide further CPU savings. Queries retrieving large result sets from an IBM DB2 Analytics Accelerator are expected to perform better in DB2 11.

Specialty Engines

An IBM System z server can be configured with optional processors known as *specialty engines (SEs)*. SEs are slightly modified standard processors that are designed to offload eligible workloads from general-purpose (GP) processors. Some of the CPU processing that would otherwise be executed on GP processors can, under certain conditions, be executed on an SE.

At the time of this writing, four specialty engines are available:

- System z Integrated Information Processor (zIIP)
- System z Application Assist Processor (zAAP)
- Integrated Facility for Linux® (IFL)
- System Assist Processor (SAP)

z/OS zIIPs can help to dramatically reduce the total cost of ownership for System z mainframes because the workload executed on them is not taken into account for software pricing. In addition, the purchase price of a zIIP is typically significantly lower than that of a standard processor.

zIIPs were introduced in 2006 as part of System z9® hardware, designed to work with Version 8 of DB2 for z/OS. Since then, the number of DB2-eligible workloads has grown steadily. DB2 10 for z/OS and DB2 11 for z/OS provide several zIIP-related improvements. DB2 for z/OS is not the only software that can leverage the ability to offload CPU to zIIPs; many software products from IBM and other vendors can take advantage of these specialty engines, as well.

DB2 10 and Specialty Engines

DB2 10 extends the scope of the zIIP-eligible workload, increasing the potential to reduce TCO through the following improvements:

- The ability to offload 100 percent of prefetch and deferred write engines. This enhancement is significant for index compression and insert index I/O parallelism.

- The ability to offload 99 percent of RUNSTATS CPU (with no additional parameters).

- In z/OS V1R11, DFSORT support for additional zIIP redirect for DB2 utilities.

- Improvements to the parsing process of XML schema validation, including eligibility of 100 percent of the new validation parser and the ability to offload to zIIP, zAAP, or zAAP on zIIP.

- Increased zIIP eligibility for DRDA® workloads, from 53 percent to 60 percent.

- Certain DBM1 processes.

- Prefetch I/Os (reported as DBM1 service request block, or SRB).

- Deferred write I/Os (reported as DBM1 SRB).

- Stored procedures written in SQL PL.

Native SQL stored procedures, introduced in DB2 9, are an excellent performance choice. They perform faster that WLM address space established stored procedures. Native SQL stored procedures are zIIP-eligible, but only when called from a distributed application using DRDA and TCP/IP.

DB2 11 and Specialty Engines

DB2 11 provides more zIIP exploitation by increasing the zIIP offload for system task SRB processing in the MSTR and DBM1 address spaces. The zIIP eligibility for IBM utilities is increased as well: RUNSTATS with distribution statistics up to 80 percent and an additional 30 percent for inline statistics.

Estimating zIIP Savings

A zIIP processor is not required to evaluate its potential benefits. The SYS1.PARMLIB parameter PROJECTCPU=YES enables z/OS to collect specialty engine usage as if a specialty engine were installed. This projection capability can be run at any time, including in a production environment. PROJECTCPU can help to determine the number of zAAP and zIIP engines required to satisfy a specific customer's workload.

With the projected usage information, you can identify which portion of the CPU would be executed on a zIIP processor. For example, consider the daily CPU profile for the data warehouse LPAR shown in Figure 9. This LPAR does not have zIIP engines.

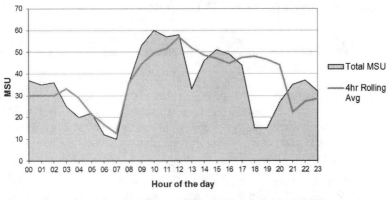

Figure 9: Daily CPU profile for a data warehouse LPAR

This chart is built using the SMF record Type 72 (RMF workload activity), and it shows the CPU used by the entire workload, DB2 and non-DB2, running in the LPAR. After activation of the PROJECTCPU z/OS parameter, the same records contains the details of the specialty engine eligible CPU executed in a general-purpose processor that would be otherwise executed in a specialty engine if available.

By subtracting the projected CPU from the total CPU used, you can model the new general-purpose CPU utilization if zIIPs with enough capacity were available in the LPAR. This information can be used to estimate a new MSU 4-hour rolling average (Figure 10). zIIP CPU time is not accounted in the MSU 4-hour rolling average.

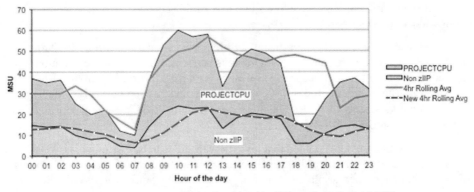

Figure 10: Projected CPU utilization with zIIPs available in the LPAR

The potential to reduce TCO by lowering CPU utilization-related costs is clear in this example. A DB2 data warehousing partition with distributed access to DB2 would be able to offload up to 60 percent of the DB2 CPU to zIIP processors.

Special Considerations for High zIIP Utilization

> **IMPORTANT:** zIIP engines can help improve your mainframe infrastructure and reduce TCO, but they cannot be always considered exactly like general-purpose processors.

Configurations where the number of zIIPs is low compared with the number of standard processors are not uncommon. This imbalance is not necessarily a problem, provided the available number of zIIPs is enough to handle the eligible workload. Nevertheless, given the trend of ever-increasing eligible workloads, the stress on zIIP engines tends to grow over time.

z/OS dispatches eligible workload to zIIPs for execution. In cases where the zIIP is too busy, the zIIP can call for help from standard processors to complete a piece of work. When the system parameter IIPHONORPRIORITY is set to YES, a standard processor can run zIIP-eligible work if called by a zIIP processor. This portion of CPU is often referred to as specialty engine eligible processor time executed on a standard processor. This time is reported on RMF records, for example, and can be used as a capacity planning metric because it indicates that the system may benefit from more zIIP capacity. When a zIIP has to ask for help from standard processors, the cost-effectiveness of the overall system suffers.

Although zIIPs can offload eligible workloads to standard processors, calling in this assistance can slow down the workload. The system parameter ZIIPAWMT specifies an Alternate Wait Management (AWM) value for zIIPs. By default (that is, when HIPERDISPATCH=YES, a recommended system parameter value for performance), this means that a transaction may have to wait up to 3.2 milliseconds before it receives help from standard processors.

Some users have reported significant performance degradation with DB2 10 for z/OS for processes that ran smoothly in previous versions of DB2. This degradation is a consequence of too little zIIP capacity as well as the delays incurred when the zIIPs require help from standard processors. This impact would be even more dramatic if IIPHONORPRIORITY were set to NO, which prevents the zIIPs from receiving assistance from standard processors.

The potential problems related to a low zIIP capacity can be exacerbated by DB2 10's capacity to offload more CPU to zIIP engines. There are a few workarounds to this situation, but the proper design decision is to add more zIIP capacity to the LPAR.

Experience shows that it is a best practice to keep zIIP utilization at approximately 50 percent, or less, to avoid processing delays. For DB2 SQL-intensive LPARs (such as a data warehouse environment), the best performance is obtained when the number of zIIPs matches the number of standard processors.

DB2 and zAAP on zIIP

The z Application Assist Processor (zAAP) specialty engines are similar to zIIPs, but they are dedicated to running specific Java® and XML workloads on z/OS. Version 1.11

of z/OS introduced a feature that lets users run zIIP- and zAAP-eligible workloads on installed zIIP processors. This feature is enabled through the use of the ZAAPZIIP keyword in the IEASYS*xx* member of SYS1.PARMLIB. When ZAAPZIIP is set to YES, zAAP-eligible work is able to run on an available zIIP processor when no zAAP processors are present.

zAAP on zIIP is an excellent opportunity for users without enough zAAP- or zIIP-eligible workload to justify the zIIP acquisition ROI.

DB2 for z/OS can leverage the TCO advantages of zAAP on zIIP. The IBM white papers *WebSphere Application Server for z/OS: The Value of Co-Location* (WP101476) and *The Value of Co-Location: Update* (WP101476-2) describe the benefits for a workload using the cross-memory DB2 JDBC Type 2 driver compared with the DB2 JDBC Type 4 driver. This study compares DB2 9 versus DB2 10 and the DB2 JDBC Type 2 driver versus the DB2 JDBC Type 4 driver performances. This document has summarized the effect of two areas of benefit:

- The CPU benefits associated with JDBC type 2, which uses cross-memory technology. This eliminates the CPU associated with the TCP stack and DB2 DDF.
- The benefits associated with DB2 z/OS V10 as compared with DB2 z/OS V9.1.

Table 1 summarizes the comparison of CPU seconds consumed during the testing.

	Type 2 DB2 V10	Type 4 DB2 V9.1	T2/V10 benefit	% T2/V10 benefit
General-purpose CPU	979.92	1111.68	131.76	11.85%
Specialty engine	1605.60	2038.68	433.08	21.24%
Total CPU time	2585.52	3150.36	564.84	17.93%

Table 1: Comparison of Type 2 and Type 4 driver CPU utilization during testing

The study assumes an environment where zAAP is available or where zAAP on zIIP is enabled. The overall conclusion is that DB2 10 and DB2 JDBC Type 2 are the best option, for the scenario described in these papers, because of the CPU and co-location benefits.

IMPORTANT: IBM zEnterprise EC12 is planned to be the last System z server to offer support for zAAP processors. IBM plans to continue support for running zAAP workloads on zIIP processors.

Reducing TCO with Better Performance

Improved DB2 performance can reduce total cost of ownership by enabling applications to deliver fast, consistent response times without the need for more CPU capacity. Good performance can yield benefits that are difficult to measure but can provide priceless competitive advantages. Examples are customer satisfaction and the capacity to absorb seasonal influences without service degradation or the need for additional resources.

After migration, DB2 10 for z/OS and DB2 11 for z/OS provide substantial CPU and performance benefits. Better performance can be obtained *out of the box*, by mere migration and REBIND, as well as by investing resources in exploiting each version's new and enhanced features (Figure 11). Some of the benefits that require application changes are hash access path, index include columns, and inline large objects.

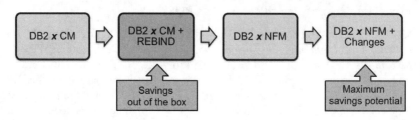

Figure 11: DB2 10 for z/OS "performance" migration path

Identifying Better Performance Opportunities

Existing applications can often be tuned to obtain better performance. When looking for performance opportunities, keep in mind the *Pareto principle*. This principle, also known as the 80–20 rule, states that roughly 80 percent of the effects come from 20 percent of the causes.

The Pareto principle usually applies well to DB2 performance. In DB2 terms, it is common to find that 80 percent of CPU utilization, locking problems, or scalability issues is produced by 20 percent of the applications. Identifying the 20 percent of applications that are of interest (from a performance point of view) lets us focus our tuning efforts. A highly effective way to define the performance focus is to look for the "top" consumers— for example, the top *x* CPU consumers, the top *y* most often executed applications, or the top *z* most active users.

The 80–20 rule usually applies to performance tuning efforts, as well. It is common to observe that 20 percent of the efforts produces 80 percent of the performance benefits. This fact is often used to look for "quick wins" or "sweet spots"—performance opportunities that have the potential to provide substantial benefits with low investment.

The *law of diminishing returns* also applies to DB2 performance tuning. This law states that a process will eventually yield to a point where additional efforts result in diminished benefits. In other words, over-tuning is not beneficial. Even though DB2 performance tuning and monitoring constitute a never-ending process, you have to stop tuning an application when the optimization efforts overcome the performance benefits.

It is essential to understand your workload profile before trying to calculate how total cost of ownership can be reduced by performance improvements. Using DB2 statistics and accounting information, in combination with RMF type 72 records, for example, it is possible to understand the resource utilization during a business period.

Figure 12 shows how CPU, measured in millions of service units, is used in a typical day in a financial institution.

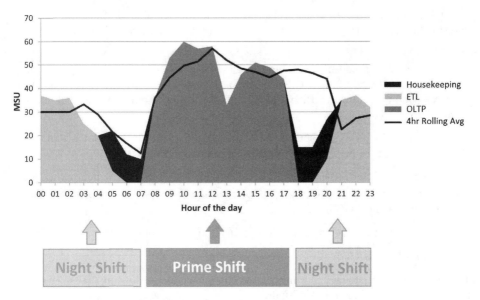

Figure 12: Daily CPU profile in a financial institution

The chart distinguishes the three main DB2 workloads: online transaction processing, housekeeping jobs, and extract, transform, and load (ETL) processes. Each one of these workloads requires specific considerations when looking for performance opportunities. Their contributions to the MSU 4-hour rolling average are also different.

Because of these inherent differences, it is a common, and good, practice to split the analysis into two or more periods. For example, the figure shows the workload split between night shift, which is characterized mostly by batch processes, and prime shift, which consists of mostly online transactions.

DB2 instrumentation is essential in this context. The DB2 accounting and statistics records are the basis of performance analysis. Consider starting these DB2 traces for continuous monitoring:

- Accounting classes 1, 2, 3, 7, and 8 with destination SMF
- Statistics classes 1, 3, 4, 5, and 6 with destination SMF

Specific performance monitoring or problem determination may require additional traces. Some performance traces may incur a performance impact and should be started only when needed.

A top-down DB2 accounting analysis approach is often effective in finding performance opportunities. Start by looking at the highest level, and then increase the level of detail. An accounting report by CONNECTION TYPE is a convenient starting point. Follow up by looking at more details for the relevant connection type—at plan or authorization ID level, for example.

In DB2 accounting, the Class 1 elapsed time shows the duration of the accounting interval. Also known as application time, it includes the time spent in DB2 and in the application.

The Class 2 elapsed time counts only the time spent in the DB2 address space during the accounting interval. It represents the sum of the times from any entry into DB2 until the corresponding exit from DB2. Class 2 elapsed time is also referred to as the time spent in DB2.

The Class 3 elapsed time counts wait time, including I/O, lock, and latch wait time. "Not accounted" time is the non-identified time spent in DB2.

Common DB2 performance bottlenecks are CPU, I/O (including synchronous I/O and logging), concurrency (locking), and storage (insufficient virtual storage and DBM1 constraint below the 2 GB bar).

As a starting point, calculate the "not in DB2 time" as follows:

Not in DB2 time = Class 1 – Class 2

The result will indicate whether further investigation should be done in DB2 or in the application logic, as illustrated in Figure 13.

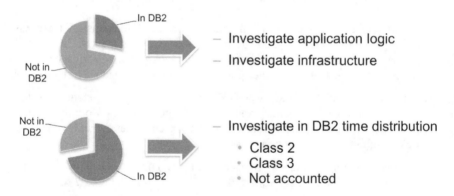

Figure 13: Investigating "not in DB2" versus "in DB2" time distribution

If most of the time is in DB2, you need to understand where the time is spent. This is a basic requirement for effective performance tuning. The time in DB2 is spent on using CPU, on waiting, or on not accounted time. The next steps in the investigation depend on the distribution of these three times.

Don't forget to verify the impact of external resources on the DB2 performance analysis. A z/OS LPAR is commonly shared by many applications, processes, and users. Effective DB2 tuning is possible only if the underlying system is well equipped to support the workload. A system issue, such as lack of CPU capacity or an incorrect Workload Manager definition, can have a significant impact on applications that can hardly be compensated for by proper tuning, good DB2 physical design, or application logic changes.

An impact analysis can help to put the performance opportunities in perspective and to focus on those with more potential for an organization. The example in Figure 14 shows a classification of opportunities by business impact versus implementation effort.

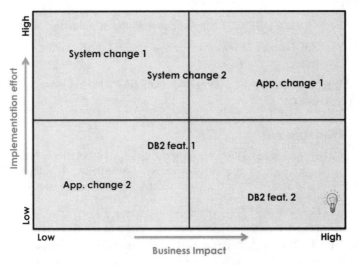

Figure 14: Impact analysis

Opportunities with low implementation effort and high business impact, also known as *quick wins* or *sweet spots*, have the potential to provide a high value in a short time with fewer efforts. Those with high implementation effort and high business impact are opportunities that can provide significant value but may not be not directly applicable.

Getting Better Performance with REBIND

The advantages of REBIND are many. Better performance is probably the most important. For example, a runtime overhead is involved in running a package bound in a previous version of DB2. Obtaining the CPU and memory advantages of a new DB2 release, as well as the benefits that may come with software maintenance, requires REBIND. You also need REBIND to gain the potential benefits of a new access path with updated DB2 statistics.

In addition, some system restrictions may impose the need for REBIND. For example, only packages bound after or in DB2 9 can be used with DB2 11.

Nevertheless, the advantages of and the need for REBIND must be balanced with the risks of access path degradation. Many organizations have adopted a conservative approach and avoid REBIND unless mandatory. Unfortunately, this policy implies a missed opportunity to get the most out of DB2 for z/OS.

DB2 has been adding features that help users to BIND and to REBIND in a safe way. For example, DB2 9's PLAN MANAGEMENT support (PLANMGMT subsystem parameter) helps users "fall back" to a previous instance of a package should an access path change cause a problem. DB2 10 enhances this support with the addition of new DB2 catalog tables and new BIND/REBIND options. DB2 11 continues the trend in this area with these enhancements:

- Further PLAN MANAGEMENT capabilities with the introduction of APREUSE(WARN)

- BIND and DDL break-in option on persistent DB2 threads with RELEASE(DEALLOCATE) packages

- The option to specify the package compatibility level behavior for static SQL (APPLCOMPAT)

DB2 Plan Management

PLAN MANAGEMENT, also referred to as access path stability, specifies whether DB2 saves historical information about the access paths for SQL statements, so you have the option to fall back to a previous version of the access path in case of performance degradation after REBIND.

PLAN MANAGEMENT imposes no performance impact at run time. It can be used when migrating to DB2 10. It provides safer mass REBIND strategies and can promote safer and easier mass REBIND campaigns when migrating to a new DB2 release.

At REBIND PACKAGE, DB2 for z/OS saves old PACKAGE copies in the DB2 SPT01 and catalog tables. Monitor SPT01 space utilization, especially with the EXTENDED option. DB2 10's APRETAINDUP(NO) REBIND option saves old copies only when they differ from the active copy.

The PLAN MANAGEMENT policy value can be:

- OFF. DB2 does not save access path information.

- BASIC. DB2 keeps information about the current access path and one additional access path, known as the previous access path. BASIC is the default in DB2 9.

- EXTENDED. DB2 saves information about the current and two additional access paths, known as the previous and original copies. EXTENDED is the default in DB2 10.

Figure 15 shows the BASIC policy in action. At REBIND, the CURRENT package copy becomes the PREVIOUS copy. The prior PREVIOUS copy is lost, and the newly created package becomes the CURRENT copy.

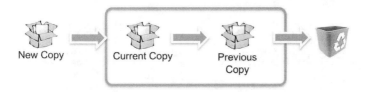

Figure 15: PLANMGMT(BASIC) policy

Figure 16 shows the EXTENDED policy in action. At REBIND, the CURRENT package copy becomes the PREVIOUS copy. The prior PREVIOUS copy is lost. If an ORIGINAL copy does not exist, the old CURRENT copy becomes the ORIGINAL copy as well; otherwise, the ORIGINAL copy is not altered. The newly created package becomes the CURRENT copy.

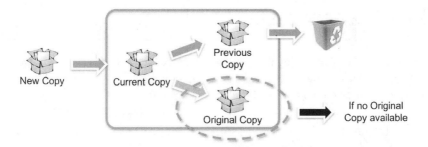

Figure 16: PLANMGMT(EXTENDED) policy

The following REBIND command shows the use of the PLANMGMT option EXTENDED:

```
REBIND PACKAGE(CRISCOLL.PCKGCRO)   -
    OWNER(PDB2)                    -
    QUALIFIER(PDB2)                -
    EXPLAIN(YES)                   -
    REOPT(NONE)                    -
    PLANMGMT(EXTENDED)
```

To revert to a previous package copy, you use the REBIND option SWITCH. Possible SWITCH values are:

- **SWITCH(PREVIOUS).** DB2 toggles the CURRENT and PREVIOUS packages. The CURRENT copy takes the place of the PREVIOUS copy, and the existing PREVIOUS copy takes the place of the CURRENT copy. Any existing ORIGINAL copy remains unchanged.

- **SWITCH(ORIGINAL).** DB2 replaces the CURRENT copy with the ORIGINAL copy; the CURRENT copy replaces the PREVIOUS copy. The existing PREVIOUS copy is lost. The existing ORIGINAL copy remains unchanged.

Figure 17 illustrates these two options.

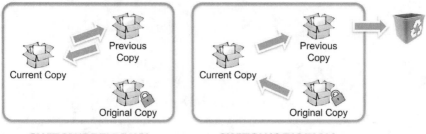

| SWITCH(PREVIOUS) | SWITCH(ORIGINAL) |

Figure 17: SWITCH(PREVIOUS) vs. SWITCH(ORIGINAL)

This example shows the use of SWITCH(ORIGINAL) in a REBIND command:

```
REBIND PACKAGE(CRISCOLL.PCKGCRO)  -
  SWITCH(ORIGINAL)
```

In DB2 10, the DB2 catalog table SYSIBM.SYSPACKCOPY contains a row for every saved package. The following SQL can be used to investigate SYSPACKAGE-like information for previous and original package copies.

```
SELECT
SUBSTR(COLLID,1,10) AS COLLID ,SUBSTR(NAME,1,10) AS NAME ,LASTUSED
  ,VALID ,OPERATIVE ,COPYID ,PLANMGMT
FROM SYSIBM.SYSPACKAGE
WHERE COLLID = 'CRISCOLL' AND NAME = 'PCKGCRO'
UNION ALL
SELECT
SUBSTR(COLLID,1,10) AS COLLID ,SUBSTR(NAME,1,10) AS NAME ,LASTUSED
  ,VALID ,OPERATIVE ,COPYID ,PLANMGMT
FROM SYSIBM.SYSPACKCOPY
WHERE COLLID = 'CRISCOLL' AND NAME = 'PCKGCRO'
WITH UR;


---------+---------+--------+---------+---------+-------+---------+-------
COLLID     NAME       LASTUSED     VALID  OPERATIVE    COPYID  PLANMGMT
---------+---------+--------+---------+---------+-------+---------+-------
CRISCOLL   PCKGCRO    2012-12-28 Y       Y                 0 E
CRISCOLL   PCKGCRO    2012-07-27 Y       Y                 1 E
CRISCOLL   PCKGCRO    2012-03-01 Y       Y                 2 E
DSNE610I NUMBER OF ROWS DISPLAYED IS 3
```

The COPYID value indicates which package copy was used:

- 1 = PREVIOUS copy
- 2 = ORIGINAL copy
- 0 = CURRENT copy

DB2 11 APREUSE(WARN) Enhancement

DB2 10 introduced the BIND/REBIND option APREUSE. This option tells DB2 to try to reuse a previous access path for an SQL statement during BIND or REBIND. DB2 10 allows two different values:

- **APREUSE(NONE).** DB2 does not try to reuse previous access paths for statements in the package. This value is the default.

- **APREUSE(ERROR).** DB2 tries to reuse the previous access paths for SQL statements. If statements in the package cannot reuse the previous access path, REBIND fails, and no new package is created. Processing continues for the next package.

This feature is similar to having DB2 automatically use optimization hints. As such, there is no guaranty of success for every case. For example, if an index that is needed to apply a previous access path is missing, access path reuse will not work.

APREUSE provides an effective way to have packages gain the benefits of the DB2 10 run-time and real storage advantages while keeping a well-known access path. APREUSE exploits the information stored in the Explain Data Block (EDB) that was introduced in DB2 9. Only packages bound in DB2 9 or later can take advantage of APREUSE.

APREUSE(ERROR) is not always the best solution, and users have wanted an intermediate option between APREUSE(NONE) and APREUSE(ERROR)—one that would result in a new package even if the previous access path could not be used, and that would provide diagnostic information about access path reuse failures.

In DB2 10, APREUSE hints are applied at the query block level. If hints could not be applied for all the query blocks in a given SQL statement, the resulting access path could be less than optimal or even show access path regression. DB2 11 changes the granularity at which hints are applied. If DB2 cannot apply a hint for a statement, the entire hint is discarded at the statement level, and DB2 reoptimizes the statement in its entirety. This change lets DB2 11 extend the APREUSE functionality by adding the option WARN.

With APREUSE(WARN), DB2 tries to reuse the previous access paths for SQL statements in the package, but REBIND is not prevented when they cannot be reused. Instead, DB2 generates a new access path for the SQL statement and ignores the previous access path. While APREUSE(ERROR) operates on a package boundary, APREUSE(WARN) can be seen as operating on a statement boundary.

With DB2 11, users can mass REBIND a DB2 environment and be notified about those packages on which access path reuse was not possible. As with HINTS, it is to be expected that a small percentage of the packages will not apply. With APREUSE(WARN), you get a new package and the notification that reuse was not possible. Not being able to reuse an access path is not necessarily an issue, because the new access path could actually be better than the previous one. An exploration of the PLAN_TABLE information can help you decide whether to let the package run with the new access path or to switch back to a previous package. The latter possibility requires the use of the PLANMGMT bind option.

DB2 11 improves the diagnostic information made available for cases in which reuse cannot be applied. When you use APREUSE in combination with EXPLAIN(YES) or EXPLAIN(ONLY), DB2 populates the PLAN_TABLE with access path information. In DB2 11, the PLAN_TABLE accurately describes the valid new access path even in case of reuse failure, regardless of whether APREUSE(ERROR) or APREUSE(WARN) is specified.

DB2 11 RELEASE(DEALLOCATE) Optimization

The BIND option RELEASE(DEALLOCATE) can reduce CPU for some applications, but there are some concerns related to its utilization. It is therefore a performance best practice to apply RELEASE(DEALLOCATE) selectively and to measure the impacts on application performance and concurrency. For example, REBIND and DDL operations may experience timeout with persistent threads using RELEASE(DEALLOCATE), especially when applied to local connections such as CICS or IMS transactions. DB2 11 alleviates this concern by supporting BIND and DDL operations to break in persistent threads.

Before DB2 11, for applications running with RELEASE(DEALLOCATE), the accumulation of objects referenced in storage could impact thread footprint and CPU usage as the number of objects per thread increased. DB2 11 provides optimizations in the RELEASE(DEALLOCATE) processing and automatically tracks resource and lock usage. To provide consistently good performance, DB2 11 frees resources and locks held by packages that touch a large number of objects once internal thresholds are reached. This change relaxes the concerns around the use of RELEASE(DEALLOCATE).

DB2 11 Application Compatibility and APPLCOMPAT

Some applications might behave differently or receive an error when they try to use DB2 11 functions and features. For this reason, DB2 11 provides the ability to run individual applications as in DB2 10 once you migrate to DB2 11 NFM. The BIND/REBIND option APPLCOMPAT specifies the package compatibility level behavior for static SQL. For dynamic SQL, the behavior is determined by the APPLICATION COMPATIBILITY special register. The compatibility level can be:

- V10R1. Applications run with the features and behavior of DB2 10.

- V11R1. Applications run with the features and behavior of DB2 11.

DB2 11 application compatibility gives users a safer migration path. It relaxes the need to review every application's functionality before migrating to DB2 11 and helps guarantee that no behavior changes will happen with the new DB2. While this option isolates applications from release incompatibilities, it also prevents them from getting some of the SQL advantages of DB2 11.

Application compatibility can be applied at the package level. When a potential application or SQL incompatibility is fixed, you can change the APPLCOMPAT value to V11R1 to let an individual application be able to exploit the new options of DB2 11.

Case Study: Performance Benefits of REBIND

REBIND can provide performance benefits in many ways, but organizations often do not REBIND as a way to protect applications from possible access path degradation. The risks of degraded performance can be minimized by exploiting PLAN MANAGEMENT. Working with PLAN MANAGEMENT provides a fallback option to a previous access path in case of issues. There is no runtime impact for packages bound with PLAN MANAGEMENT.

A financial institution avoiding REBIND decides to exploit PLAN MANAGEMENT to explore the potential benefits of a mass REBIND campaign. As a first exercise, the user decides to REBIND all packages used in the OLTP workload window.

In DB2 9, the following query provides the distribution of the packages by RELBOUND, the release when the package was bound or rebound.

```
SELECT
RELBOUND, COUNT(*)
FROM  SYSIBM.SYSPACKAGE
WHERE VALID <> 'N'
  AND OPERATIVE <> 'N'
GROUP BY RELBOUND
WITH UR;
```

DB2 10 introduced the LASTUSED column in SYSIBM.SYSPACKAGE to track the date when a package was last used. This information can be extremely handy to safely free unused packages or to decide that a REBIND of a package may be useful. The following example uses the LASTUSED column in a query.

```
SELECT
RELBOUND, COUNT(*)
FROM  SYSIBM.SYSPACKAGE
WHERE VALID <> 'N'
  AND OPERATIVE <> 'N'
  WHERE LASTUSED >=
  (CURRENT_DATE - 1 MONTH)
GROUP BY RELBOUND
WITH UR;
```

The RELBOUND distribution for this company revealed that although the organization is running DB2 10, only 35 percent of the packages were bound in this release. Almost 49 percent of packages were last bound in DB2 9, and 16 percent in DB2 8.

The organization decided to mass REBIND all the packages using PLANMGMT(EXTENDED), executing a mass REORG and RUNSTATS campaign in preparation for the changes. Figure 18 shows the performance results, comparing CPU utilization and number of SQL transactions per hour before and after REBIND.

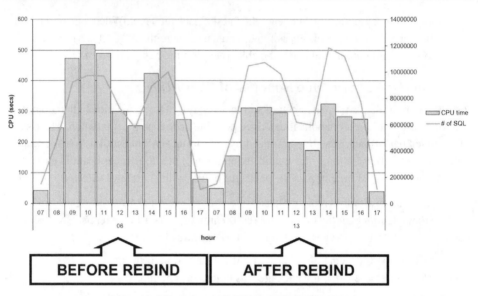

Figure 18: Effect of mass REBIND on total DB2 CPU time

As a result of the mass REBIND of more than 2,000 DB2 packages, the CPU utilization is visibly reduced and the transaction throughput is higher.

Two frequently used packages went wrong. The new packages included a multiple-index access path that had row ID (RID) list failures. This performance issue was quickly fixed by switching back to the previous packages. Further investigation ended up adding the REOPT option to REBIND for these packages.

DB2 EXPLAIN At a Glance

DB2 EXPLAIN provides valuable information to help you understand the optimizer choices and tune application performance. Among the many available EXPLAIN options are:

- **BIND/REBIND with EXPLAIN(YES).** Generates a new access path, populates PLAN_TABLE, and creates a new package

- **BIND/REBIND with EXPLAIN(ONLY).** Generates a new access path, populates PLAN_TABLE, but *does not* create a new package

- **EXPLAIN PLAN (i.e., SPUFI).** Generates a new access path and populates PLAN_TABLE

- **EXPLAIN PACKAGE.** *Does not* generate a new access path; extracts the existing access path from the package and populates PLAN_TABLE

DB2 10 High-Performance DBATs

DB2 10 provides valuable performance improvements for distributed applications, including improved return to client result sets, enhanced support for native SQL PL procedures, extended correlation token, virtual and real storage improvements, and LOBs and XML materialization avoidance.

One of the most relevant changes is the introduction of high-performance database access threads (DBATs). DB2 10 high-performance DBAT support reduces CPU consumption by supporting the BIND option RELEASE(DEALLOCATE) for distributed access to DB2. These enhancements save CPU by avoiding repeated package allocation/ deallocation and avoiding acquiring and releasing parent (IS, IX) locks frequently.

The more noticeable CPU reduction is expected for short transactions, typically OLTP workloads. No benefit is achieved for ACTIVE threads (CMSTATS=ACTIVE), nor for applications running with the REBIND option KEEPDYNAMIC YES.

Table 2 summarizes the observed performance results during controlled OLTP benchmark tests. It compares DB2 9 with DB2 10 results out of the box, then shows further savings achieved when running DB2 10 with RELEASE(DEALLOCATE). The times shown are the total CPU time (in microseconds) per transaction, that is:

Total CPU = DB2 System Services Address Space + Database Services Address Space + IRLM + DDF Address Space CPU

Workload	DB2 9 CPU (ms)	DB2 10 CPU (ms)	Savings	DB2 10 DEALLOCATE CPU (ms)	Savings
SQL ODBC/CLI: Dynamic SQL	2114	1997	5.5%	1918	9.3%
JDBC: Dynamic SQL	2152	2017	6.3%	1855	13.8%
SQLJ: Static SQL	1899	1761	11.9%	1668	16.6%
Stored procedures in SQLJ with static SQL	1768	1642	6.7%	1550	11.9%

Table 2: OLTP benchmark test results

DB2 provides the –MODIFY DDF PKGREL command to activate or deactivate the distributed RELEASE(DEALLOCATE) option support. The –MODIFY DDF command's PKGREL option specifies whether DB2 ignores the BIND options of packages used for remote client processing. PKGREL can be modified by two options:

- **BNDOPT.** The rules of the RELEASE bind option that were specified when the package was bound are applied. This is the default option in DB2 10.

- **COMMIT.** The rules of the RELEASE(COMMIT) bind option are applied. This is the DB2 9 (and earlier) behavior.

This example shows how to enable the honoring of the RELEASE option for distributed packages:

```
-MODIFY DDF PKGREL(BNDOPT)
```

After executing this command, DB2 outputs the following feedback in the MSTR address space.

```
STC12396 DSNL300I  -DBOA DSNLTMDF MODIFY DDF REPORT FOLLOWS:
          DSNL302I PKGREL IS SET TO BNDOPT
          DSNL301I DSNLTMDF MODIFY DDF REPORT COMPLETE
```

To disable, use the following syntax; this overlays the distributed package's RELEASE option and causes DB2 to apply the RELEASE(COMMIT) behavior.

```
-MODIFY DDF PKGREL(COMMIT)
```

The –DIS DDF DETAIL command contains the DSNL106I message, which reports the current status of the PKGREL option. The following –DIS DDF DETAIL command output shows that the current status for PKGREL is COMMIT in this system.

```
DSNL080I  -DBCM DSNLTDDF DISPLAY DDF REPORT FOLLOWS:
DSNL081I STATUS=STARTD
DSNL082I LOCATION            LUNAME            GENERICLU
DSNL083I DBCM                OVERIJS.TOTDBCM   -NONE
DSNL084I TCPPORT=12345 SECPORT=12346 RESPORT=12347 IPNAME=-NONE
DSNL085I IPADDR=::10.50.1.1
DSNL086I SQL    DOMAIN=www.molaro.be
DSNL090I DT=I CONDBAT=  10000 MDBAT=  200
DSNL092I ADBAT=    0 QUEDBAT=    0 INADBAT=    0 CONQUED=      0
DSNL093I DSCDBAT=    0 INACONN=    1
DSNL105I CURRENT DDF OPTIONS ARE:
DSNL106I PKGREL = COMMIT
DSNL099I DSNLTDDF DISPLAY DDF REPORT COMPLETE
```

Running distributed applications with RELEASE(DEALLOCATE) improves performance in many cases. However, it could become difficult to execute some operations, such as DDL, on objects allocated by the workload.

IMPORTANT: The BIND/REBIND option RELEASE(DEALLOCATE) may create concurrency problems. Plan for a gradual implementation and monitor impacts.

Reducing TCO Through Storage Savings

The worldwide growth of information has been increasing steadily for many years. In 2007, the amount of information created, captured, or replicated exceeded available storage for the first time. With big data, this scenario is certainly not going to revert.

As an illustration, consider the storage requirements to support the insert of a simple 9-byte DB2 table row as illustrated in Figure 19.

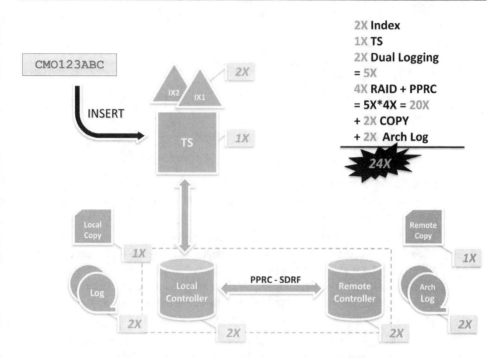

Figure 19: Storage required for a simple table insert

The data has to be saved once in the table space containing the table. Assuming that the row's columns are part of two indexes, the data has to be stored two times more. The usual dual-logging system then requires storing the data two times more. At this point, the original data has to be written five times already. Normally, disk storage is replicated to a remote data center using replication techniques such as peer-to-peer remote copy (PPRC). Local storage is mirrored with some form of redundant array of independent disks (RAID). As shown in this example, a commonly found configuration, the inserted data is stored 24 times.

Several DB2 catalog tables can be used to analyze storage space utilization. For example, you can create reports about the number of kilobytes of DASD storage allocated using the SPACE and SPACEF columns of table SYSIBM.SYSINDEXES, SYSIBM.SYSTABLESPACE, SYSIBM.SYSINDEXPART, SYSIBM.SYSTABLEPART, and SYSIBM.SYSSTOGROUP.

The STOSPACE DB2 utility refreshes these columns. It determines the amount of space allocated for DB2 storage groups and their related table spaces and indexes. STOSPACE does not set a utility restrictive state on target objects, and it can run concurrently with any utility. It is also cheaper and faster to execute than RUNSTATS, so it is a better option if you are looking only for space analysis information.

This example shows how to execute the STOSPACE utility:

```
//JOBCARD
//* -------------------------
//STOSPACE EXEC PGM=DSNUTILB...
...
//SYSOUT   DD SYSOUT=*
//SYSIN    DD *
   STOSPACE STOGROUP *
/*
```

The DB2 realtime statistics tables are also a good information source. For example:

- **SYSIBM.SYSINDEXSPACESTATS.** The LASTUSED column contains the date when the index was last used for SELECT, FETCH, searched UPDATE, searched DELETE, or to enforce referential integrity constraints.

- **SYSIBM.SYSTABLESPACESTATS.** The SPACE column shows the amount of space, in kilobytes, allocated to the table space or partition; for multi-piece, linear page sets, this value is the amount of space in all data sets. The DATASIZE column provides the total number of bytes that row data occupy in the data rows or LOB rows. The UNCOMPRESSEDDATASIZE column shows the total number of bytes that a data row would have occupied if the data were not compressed.

Even if the storage cost per unit of data is decreasing, ever-increasing space demands make storage a substantial investment. The opportunities to reduce total cost of ownership related to storage can be classified in two main categories: optimizing storage utilization and dividing the data.

Optimizing storage aims to reduce the storage requirements for valuable business data. DB2 for z/OS provides several techniques to achieve this objective, including data compression, DB2 managed disk space allocation, and index compression. Rationalization of object-related storage can provide big savings as well, by removing redundant objects and reclaiming unused space, for example.

Dividing the data means exploiting DB2 features such as partitioning or creating history tables to reduce the amount of data that has to be processed by applications and housekeeping processes. The smaller the data scope, the faster and less expensive the processing.

DB2 Data Compression

In many cases, compressing the data in a table space significantly reduces the amount of disk space needed to store data. This effect can reduce TCO by lowering space requirements. Data compression can provide performance benefits, as well.

DB2 data compression and decompression are hardware-assisted. This approach helps to reduce CPU costs related to accessing and manipulating compressed data. In general, compression and decompression get faster with each new generation of System z servers, as processors get faster.

DB2 compression is a lossless compression implementation. That is, no details from the data are lost when compressing/decompressing. On the other hand, lossy compression techniques, such as that used to create JPEG images, involves losing some information each time you compress the data. With DB2 for z/OS, data is compressed in the DB2 logs, in the buffer pools, and in the data pages in both table spaces and copies.

Data compression is dictionary-based. Before getting compression results, you must create a dictionary using the LOAD or REORG utility. A missing or inadequate dictionary results in a less effective compression ratio.

Figure 20 depicts the internal changes in a table space after compression. Note the addition of the dictionary in the AFTER section of the figure.

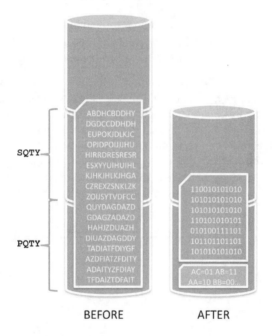

BEFORE   AFTER

Figure 20: Table space changes following compression

One dictionary is maintained per compressed table space partition. Since DB2 8, the dictionary is loaded in DB2 storage above the 2 GB bar. Nevertheless, with up to 4,096 partitions per table and sixteen 4 KB pages per dictionary, memory requirements can increase quickly when monitoring real storage utilization and system paging.

The compression ratio depends on the data characteristics. Compression can work well for large table spaces. But with small ones, compression may result in more space utilization due to the introduction of the compression dictionary. You can use the DB2-provided DSN1COMP standalone utility to estimate compression effects before compressing a table space. The following example shows the output of an execution of DSN1COMP; in this case, 25 percent of the bytes will be saved.

```
DSN1940I DSN1COMP COMPRESSION REPORT
          301  KB WITHOUT COMPRESSION
          224  KB WITH COMPRESSION
           25  PERCENT OF THE BYTES WOULD BE SAVED

        1,975  ROWS SCANNED TO BUILD DICTIONARY
        4,665  ROWS SCANNED TO PROVIDE COMPRESSION ESTIMATE
        4,096  DICTIONARY ENTRIES

           81  BYTES FOR AVERAGE UNCOMPRESSED ROW LENGTH
           52  BYTES FOR AVERAGE COMPRESSED ROW LENGTH

           16  DICTIONARY PAGES REQUIRED
          110  PAGES REQUIRED WITHOUT COMPRESSION
           99  PAGES REQUIRED WITH COMPRESSION
           10  PERCENT OF THE DB2 DATA PAGES WOULD BE SAVED
```

You can query the DB2 catalog to obtain information about the actual effectiveness of compression. For example, column PAGESAVE of SYSIBM.SYSTABLEPART provides the percentage of pages that are saved by compressing the data.

Figure 21 shows the PAGESAVE distribution for the table spaces of a DB2 for z/OS data warehousing environment. To build this chart, only COMPRESS=Y table spaces were considered. In general, this kind of environment often shows compression ratios of 50 percent or more, which can safely be considered as compression working okay for the data in these table spaces. A compression ratio below 50 percent may require attention; compression may not be effective for that data, or the dictionary may need to be re-created. PAGESAVE < 1 requires immediate review; this may indicate either that compression results in more space requirements or, more commonly, that a dictionary is missing.

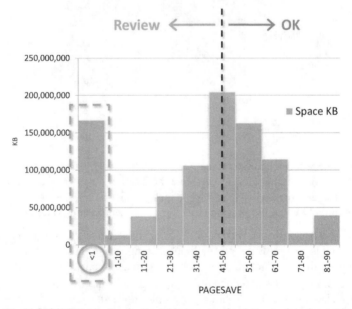

Figure 21: PAGESAVE distribution for the table spaces of a data warehousing environment

On top of space savings, DB2 data compression can provide other kinds of performance advantages. Because data is compressed in buffer pools, compression may enable storing more information within the same buffer pool size. This can make the buffer pool scanning of large amounts of data more effective or increase the buffer pool hit ratio. Compression can reduce DB2 logging and speed up taking copies.

In many cases, compressing the data in a table space significantly reduces the amount of disk space needed to store data. Nevertheless, data compression may not be the best choice for every object. Because DB2 compresses the data one record at a time, compression may be not efficient with short rows because 8 bytes of overhead are required to store each record in a data page. Even if rows compress well, there is a limit of a maximum 255 rows per page. This may result in data pages with lots of empty space, and you may end up with compression overhead but no space savings.

DB2 Managed Disk Space Allocation

Traditionally, a database administrator designs the storage characteristics of a table space and defines the primary and secondary quantities in the DDL USING block, as shown in this example:

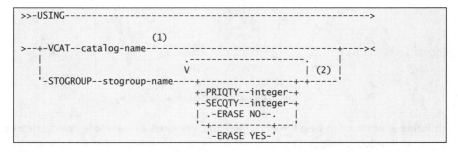

PRIQTY specifies the minimum primary space allocation, and SECQTY specifies the minimum secondary space allocation for a DB2 managed data set. This approach has been used successfully, but it requires administration and monitoring efforts. In addition, big SECQTY values may result in large quantities of unused allocated storage space.

With DB2 managed disk space allocation, DB2 can calculate the amount of space to allocate to secondary extents by using a sliding-scale algorithm. The first 127 extents are allocated in increasing size, and the remaining extents are allocated based on the initial size of the data set. If the environment is not suffering from severe DASD fragmentation, a table space should reach its dataset space limit before reaching its maximum number of extents.

Sliding scale for secondary space allocation is an optional DB2 feature. It can help to reduce TCO by simplifying the administrative tasks related to the monitoring of DB2 table space and index space extents. Because the size of the secondary extents follows the growing of the data, it can provide storage savings by keeping unused space to a minimum.

Figure 22 shows the initial space utilization of, and the effects of sliding on, an enterprise development environment. Objects used to be created using large space allocations in preparation for receiving data. With sliding allocation, unused space is reduced to a minimum.

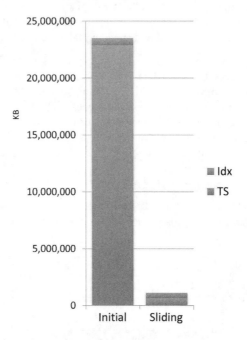

Figure 22: Effects of sliding-scale allocation of secondary space

Sliding allocation can help to save significant quantities of storage by optimizing the data pages allocated. There is no effect on data. Figure 23 shows that sliding does not change the amount of data in the object. Savings come from DB2's smarter and automatic extent management.

Case Study: Combined Effects of Data Compression and DB2 Managed Disk Space Allocation

DB2 data compression and DB2 managed disk space allocation can be combined to obtain a maximum storage space savings. This case study shows an example.

The starting point is a DB2 table holding about 10,000,000 rows. The table is supported by a partitioned table space with three partitions. Because of business needs, the data cannot be evenly distributed at the initial stage.

Figure 24 illustrates how to use the DB2 catalog tables to obtain space information about this object. SYSTABLES gives the total number of rows under CARD and the number of pages that include rows of the table under NPAGES. SYSTABLEPART shows the details per partition: the number of rows per partition under CARD, storage space utilization under SPACE, and number of data set extents under EXTENTS.

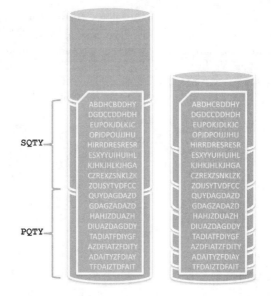

Figure 23: Object data unaffected by sliding-scale allocation

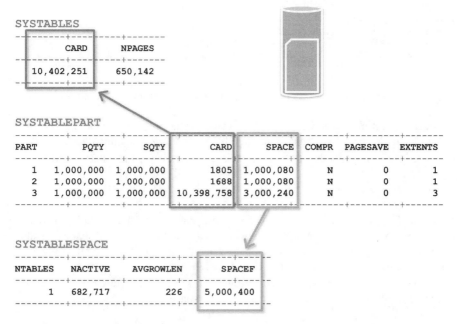

SYSTABLES

CARD	NPAGES
10,402,251	650,142

SYSTABLEPART

PART	PQTY	SQTY	CARD	SPACE	COMPR	PAGESAVE	EXTENTS
1	1,000,000	1,000,000	1805	1,000,080	N	0	1
2	1,000,000	1,000,000	1688	1,000,080	N	0	1
3	1,000,000	1,000,000	10,398,758	3,000,240	N	0	3

SYSTABLESPACE

NTABLES	NACTIVE	AVGROWLEN	SPACEF
1	682,717	226	5,000,400

Figure 24: Using the DB2 catalog tables to obtain space information about an object

Figure 25 shows the effects of altering the table space to COMPRESS=Y and creating a compression dictionary with a REORG utility. The number of rows does not change, but the average row length goes from 226 to 47 bytes as a result of compression. The number of data pages containing rows drops from 650,142 to 142,577. And the kilobytes of DASD used by the table space is reduced from 5,000,400 to 3,000,240. In this example, compression reduced the space requirements by approximately 40 percent.

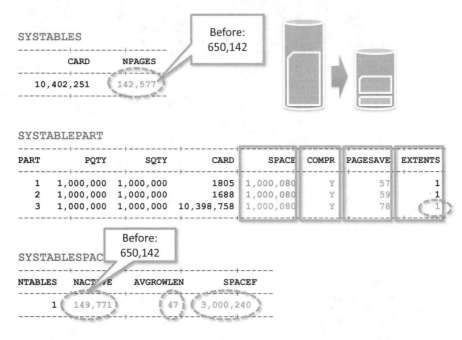

Figure 25: Using the DB2 catalog tables to show space savings after compression

Because partitions 1 and 2 are over-allocated for the amount of data they contain, altering the table space to use a sliding scale for secondary space allocation can help further reduce storage needs. PQTY and SQTY are altered to –1, and a REORG utility is required to adjust the extents. Figure 26 shows the final results. There is no impact on the number of pages, but the DASD space is reduced to 621,360 KB.

Figure 27 gives a graphical summary of these changes. In this example, the combined effects of DB2 data compression and sliding scale for secondary space allocation reduced the storage requirements by almost 90 percent without affecting the data. In addition, applications accessing the data may benefit from some of the performance advantages of data compression. DB2 utilities such as REORG and COPY may execute faster as a result of the reduced table space DASD space.

```
SYSTABLES
---------+---------+-------
      CARD      NPAGES
---------+---------+-------
  10,402,251    142,577
---------+---------+-------
```

```
SYSTABLEPART
---------+---------+---------+---------+---------+-------+---------+---------
PART      PQTY      SQTY          CARD     SPACE  COMPR  PAGESAVE  EXTENTS
---------+---------+---------+---------+---------+-------+---------+---------
  1        -1        -1          1805       720     Y        57        1
  2        -1        -1          1688       720     Y        59        1
  3        -1        -1    10,398,758    619920     Y        78       21
---------+---------+---------+---------+---------+-------+---------+---------
```

```
SYSTABLESPACE
---------+---------+---------+---------+------
NTABLES   NACTIVE   AVGROWLEN     SPACEF
---------+---------+---------+---------+------
      1    149,771          47     621,360
---------+---------+---------+---------+------
```

Figure 26: Using the DB2 catalog tables to show the impact of sliding scale

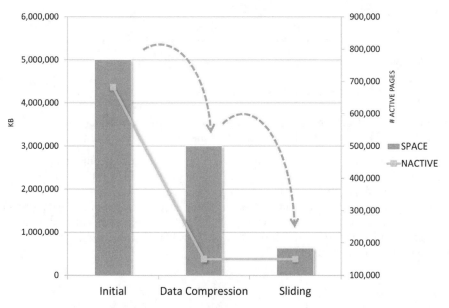

Figure 27: Combined effects of data compression and sliding scale on space

Index Compression

In DB2 data warehouse environments, it is common to take advantage of DB2 data compression to save DASD storage and reduce costs. To improve performance, extensive use of indexes is common. As a consequence of these two factors combined, it is usual to see environments where the disk storage space used by indexes is bigger than that for table spaces.

Figure 28 shows the space utilization, in kilobytes, of the table spaces and index spaces for the five biggest databases in manufacturing organization's DB2 data warehouse environment.

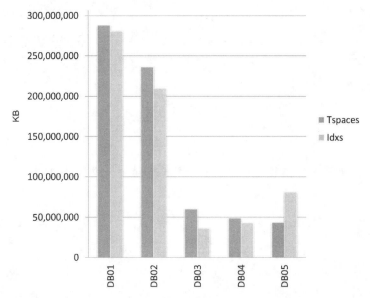

Figure 28: Space utilization in a DB2 data warehouse environment

In this case, DASD space used by indexes is almost as much as that used by table spaces, with indexes representing 48 percent of the total space requirements.

To further reduce storage requirements, DB2 introduced index compression in DB2 9. DB2 uses a hybrid compression algorithm that employs prefix compression to compress index pages. Index compression is not the same as data compression. The goal of index compression is to save index storage on disk. Compression of index data occurs on disk only and is not hardware-supported. With index compression, CPU overhead is incurred at read and write I/O execution time only. Table 3 outlines the differences between data and index compression.

	Data compression	Index compression
Technique	Ziv-Lempel hardware assisted	Prefix compression
Dictionary	Must be built before getting data compressed	Not needed, compression starts immediately
Data on disk	Compressed	Compressed
Data on DB2 log	Compressed	Not compressed
Data in buffer pool	Compressed	Not compressed
Image copies	Compressed	Not compressed

Table 3: Data compression vs. index compression

The compression ratio depends on the data and on how the columns are distributed in the index. The buffer pool choice determines the maximum disk space savings and the efficiency of memory utilization.

With index compression, DB2 stores index data on disk in 4 KB pages. The compressed data is expanded into buffer pool pages of 8 KB, 16 KB, or 32 KB. The choice of the buffer pool page size is a design decision. This selection, along with how well the index data compress, defines the efficiency of the process and the storage savings. The maximum amount of disk storage saving you can achieve when using index compression is limited by the index buffer pool:

- For 8 KB, up to 51 percent compression
- For 16 KB, up to 76 percent compression
- For 32 KB, up to 88 percent compression

The choice of an inappropriate buffer pool page size can result in either wasted buffer pool memory or wasted DASD storage.

The DB2-provided standalone utility DSN1COMP supports index compression. It can be used to estimate the space savings on disk due to index compression and to select the buffer pool size that best fits the index. This example shows the output of one execution:

```
 8  K Page Buffer Size yields a
40  % Reduction in Index Leaf Page Space
60  % of the original index's Leaf Page Space
16  % of Bufferpool Space would be unused to
    ------------------------------------------------
16  K Page Buffer Size yields a
41  % Reduction in Index Leaf Page Space
59  % of the original index's Leaf Page Space
57  % of Bufferpool Space would be unused to
    ------------------------------------------------
32  K Page Buffer Size yields a
41  % Reduction in Index Leaf Page Space
59  % of the original index's Leaf Page Space
78  % of Bufferpool Space would be unused to
```

The decision to deploy index compression should be made carefully and should be implemented on a case-by-case basis as much as possible. Because of the nature of the prefix compression algorithm, two indexes composed of the same columns but arranged in a different sequence could compress remarkably differently. In Figure 29, the printout of the VSAM pages of two compressed indexes shows that less information is stored in the page for the column sequence NAME, KEY. This index compressed more than the one with the sequence KEY, NAME.

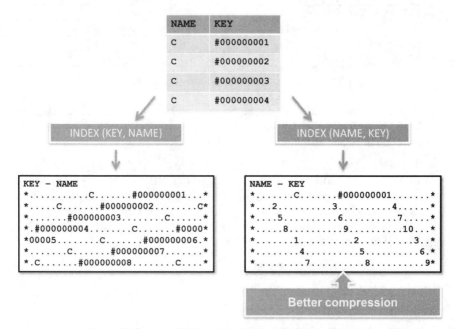

Figure 29: Impact of index column order on index compression

In general, a data warehouse environment is an excellent candidate for index compression. You may consider index compression where a reduction in index storage consumption is more beneficial than a possible increase in CPU consumption.

Index compression may not be a convenient choice for OLTP environments. However, larger index pages can be used independently of index compression. A larger index page can provide performance benefits to OLTP transactions, reducing the number of index levels and preventing index page splits.

Reducing TCO with Faster Analytics

DB2 and System z are platforms of choice for decision support environments worldwide. DB2 for z/OS has been adding warehousing- and analytics-specific functionality with each new release. Today, it is possible to build an end-to-end enterprise warehousing solution on System z that includes data extraction, transformation, load, query, and reporting functionalities.

Analytics and warehousing queries are complex, highly resource-intensive workloads that require organizations to process massive amounts of data. Big data is a reality today, and data volumes will only continue to grow. In addition, the dynamics of global competition mean that companies must leverage the information in their systems quickly to help them make smart, informed strategy decisions.

DB2 for z/OS provides capabilities that can deliver the analytics that businesses require from existing DB2 data. It can leverage existing data into faster analytics. These capabilities save the need for third-party database or new infrastructure developments and, therefore, contribute to total cost of ownership savings.

IBM DB2 Analytics Accelerators

In many situations, the speed at which analysts can understand and react to changes in a dynamic business environment is limited by the IT infrastructure's ability to process complex queries against large volumes of data. Ideally, business analytics would be unconstrained by infrastructure limitations. Organizations could leverage near-instantaneous analytics and run reports when they need them, even in real time. This is where DB2 query accelerators come into the picture.

A DB2 query accelerator is a transparent-to-the-user tool designed to boost database speed and performance. Accelerators can provide dramatic improvements in response time and reduce CPU utilization by offloading eligible queries to specifically designed hardware. They can help deliver faster, more reactive business insight by executing analytics when they are required and at high speed.

The IBM DB2 Analytics Accelerator can dramatically improve performance and reduce the cost of analytics in DB2 for z/OS environments. Available as an add-on appliance built on IBM Netezza® technology, the accelerator is designed for easy, rapid deployment. Users simply instruct DB2 to consider the query accelerator the new access path for eligible queries on eligible objects. The appliance requires very little configuration, and accelerator performance information is integrated with the usual DB2 traces.

For candidate queries, the results can be astonishing. Queries often run significantly faster than they ever have before. Response times for well-tuned queries running on current-generation traditional hardware can shrink from hours to seconds. Queries that previously ran too slowly to be useful can often be completed in minutes. As response times approach what you might expect from an OLTP environment, realtime analytics can become an everyday reality.

Potentially, a good portion of the CPU consumed by queries running in DB2 can be eliminated by offloading the query processing to the accelerator. Nevertheless, offloaded queries returning a large result set could consume a noticeable amount of CPU time in DB2. This scenario is improved with a performance enhancement introduced in DB2 11 for z/OS.

Figure 30 shows the CPU utilization and evolution of the MSU 4-hour rolling average during the execution of a data warehousing workload. This scenario is the combination of short, medium, and long intensive queries executed entirely in DB2.

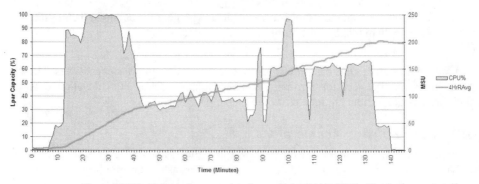

Figure 30: Workload before acceleration – Total LPAR CPU utilization

Figure 31 shows the same scenario after adding an accelerator appliance to the environment. The most complex queries were offloaded to the accelerator. As a result of the faster accelerator performance, the whole scenario was accomplished in a fraction of the original elapsed time. Most of the z/OS CPU was removed from the LPAR as queries were executed in the accelerator, reducing the impact in the MSU 4-hour rolling average, which is the usual software license cost metric.

For clarity, the chart scale is unchanged. This example shows how eligible workload can be executed faster and less expensively in the accelerator.

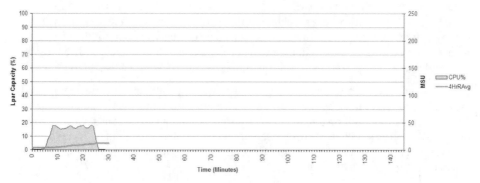

Figure 31: Workload after acceleration – Total LPAR CPU utilization

The secret of this speed resides in the highly specialized hardware and software that is tuned for serving analytics queries. The DB2 Analytics Accelerator appliance exploits massive parallel processing on dedicated CPUs, disks, and memory in a highly and linearly scalable architecture.

Figure 32 depicts the relationship between an application, DB2 for z/OS, and the accelerator. The accelerator appliance connects to z/OS and DB2 using a private network. The DB2 objects to be accelerated are defined and loaded in the accelerator using DB2 stored procedures and a graphical user interface. Once an accelerator is installed and enabled to work, the DB2 optimizer considers the appliance as a new access path and will offload SQL processing transparently when it judges that doing so would be more efficient.

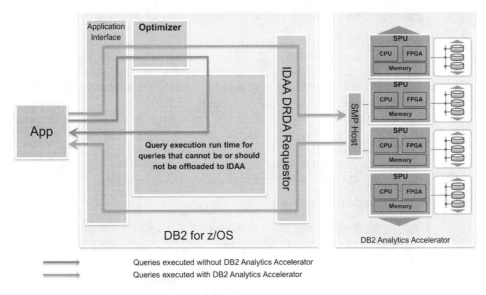

Figure 32: IBM DB2 Analytics Accelerator and DB2 for z/OS

The business value of a query accelerator resides in its close and transparent integration with DB2 and System z. You get hyper-speed analytics in the highly reliable, secure, and stable mainframe environment that you already know and love. DB2 Analytics Accelerator can not only help reduce total cost of ownership but also change how analytics are executed on DB2 and System z, the platform of choice for enterprise warehousing infrastructures.

Leverage Legacy QMF Objects

Query Management Facility™ (QMF™) was part of the initial DB2 announcement, 30 years ago in 1983. Many users have been working with QMF since the beginning of its history with DB2 for z/OS. As a result, it is common to find organizations with a long history, and an extensive catalog, of 3270-created QMF queries and reports. Nevertheless, the classic 3270 interface may not be up to the level of the graphical reporting capabilities that today's modern business require.

The evolution of the QMF target user base could be summarized as follows:

- Database administrators: QMF for TSO and High Performance Option (HPO)
- Technical users: QMF for Windows®, an extension of QMF to the desktop
- Data analysts, IT professionals: QMF for Windows/WebSphere, an extension of QMF to a web browser that also introduces graphical reporting

- Business users: QMF for Workstation/WebSphere, which provides an intuitive visual solution with a personalized, nontechnical graphical user interface and supports enhanced security, OLAP, and a variety of databases on top of DB2 for z/OS

The QMF Enterprise Edition product interoperability lets users leverage legacy QMF queries into a graphical user interface with modern reporting capabilities. For example, users can develop, edit, and run QMF queries, forms, reports, and procedures via the 3270 user interface. These QMF objects are stored in the QMF catalog within DB2 for z/OS. Users working with QMF for Workstation and WebSphere can access the same QMF catalogs and use the same object format. Queries, reports, and procedures created in QMF for TSO can be accessed, edited, and executed in QMF for Workstation and WebSphere, and vice versa. All changes made in one QMF product are immediately accessible in all other QMF products. Users can also initiate the z/OS-based execution of QMF objects from the QMF for Workstation and/or WebSphere products.

QMF advantages that can help reduce TCO include:

- QMF for Workstation eliminates the overhead of a TSO session and a QMF for TSO session during development of queries and reports, resulting in reduced z/OS CPU utilization.

- QMF High Performance Option converts QMF queries, forms, and procedures to compiled COBOL programs and DB2 COBOL stored procedures. This option can provide better performance, reduced CPU utilization, and predictable performance.

- Existing reports can be reused by the QMF family rather than being re-created in another tool, providing smooth extension of QMF reports to other areas of the business.

- The ability to use one interface and one tool to access many data sources (including DB2 for z/OS, DB2 for iSeries®, DB2 LUW, Oracle®, Microsoft SQL Server®, Microsoft Excel®, and others) increases productivity.

QMF Enterprise Edition is currently available in the form of these solutions:

- **QMF for TSO/CICS.** Supports end users who work entirely from traditional mainframe monitors to access databases in the IBM DB2 family

- **QMF HPO.** The High Performance Option for QMF for TSO/CICS is a multifaceted tool that helps database administrators manage QMF objects and increase performance in TSO and CICS environments.

- **QMF for Workstation.** Extends the key functionality of QMF for TSO/CICS on distributed platforms via a rich desktop development environment. Runs on Microsoft Windows, Linux, and Apple computer systems.

- **QMF for WebSphere.** Provides a feature set similar to that of QMF for Workstation, using a thin-client, browser-based solution and mobile device support. Runs on Windows, Linux, Solaris, AIX®, HP-UX, iSeries, z/Linux, and z/OS.

QMF for Workstation and WebSphere features that may be of interest are:

- Ad hoc and prepared queries

  o Create, edit, and reuse QMF queries

  o Apply groupings, aggregations, conditional formats, and more

  o Perform one-click export to Excel, data files, or database table

  o Perform one-click generation of reports from the data

- Tabular and graphical reports

  o Generate QMF tabular reports or graphical visual reports

  o Create highly customizable, page-based layouts

  o Draw data from any number of data sources

- QMF dashboards

  o Customized, interactive data visualizations

  o Rapid authoring model

  o Technical details

Reducing TCO with Improved Scalability

DB2 10 provides impressive reductions in memory requirements below the 2 GB bar. In prior releases, these requirements limited the concurrent number of threads and DB2 scalability. DB2 10 supports five to ten times more concurrent users per DB2 subsystem. DB2 logging and the internal DB2 serialization mechanisms (latches) have also been improved, giving overall increased throughput per DB2 subsystem.

These are examples of changes that increase the workload that a single DB2 subsystem can handle. This situation provides new consolidation opportunities where users may reduce the number of DB2 subsystems for the same workload.

DB2 subsystem consolidation and better DB2 scalability can help to reduce total cost of ownership by simplifying the IT infrastructure and reducing the data center footprint. DB2 consolidation can yield lower administrative and staff costs.

DB2 10 Throughput Enhancements

When data becomes unpredictably volatile, or when the amount of data increases, there can be performance problems related to throughput and bottleneck issues. This situation is often observed during nightly batch jobs. Many organizations are constrained in that they must wait for critical nightly batch processing to end before being able to begin their business day processing (OLTP). If the end of the batch process is delayed, it means a late start to the daytime activity. Depending on the company and its business activity, this service degradation can have a large financial impact.

DB2 10 can improve the throughput of data-intensive processes. Changes such as logging enhancements, latching contention relief, dynamic prefetch enhancement, and

I/O parallelism for index updates provide better performance, resulting in an improved throughput without the need to change existing applications.

From a performance point of view, mass insert applications need particular attention. The DB2 10 insert performance improvements help improve mass insert performance. The observed performance benefits vary with the workload characteristics.

Some of the biggest improvements were observed for high-volume, concurrent insert processes in data sharing environments. MEMBER CLUSTER support for universal table spaces is made available in DB2 10 NFM. This feature can help improve insert performance in data sharing environments.

Out-of-the-box enhancements related to insert performance include space search improvement, index I/O parallelism, log latch contention reduction and faster COMMIT processing, support for MEMBER CLUSTER in universal table spaces, and LRSN spin loop avoidance.

DB2 latching is used for short-term serialization of DB2 resources such as storage or control blocks, pages in buffer pools, or log write output buffer pages. Latches are usually very inexpensive to acquire. Under heavy load, they can become a bottleneck. The most common source of problems are DB2 log contention (in latch class 19) and prefetch latch or EDM LRU chain latch (included in latch class 24).

Most DB2 latches that could impact scalability were enhanced in DB2 10. This list summarizes some of the areas that were improved:

- LC12. Global transaction ID serialization
- LC14. Buffer manager serialization
- LC19. Log write in both data sharing and non data sharing
- LC24. EDM thread storage serialization
- LC24. Buffer manager serialization
- LC25. EDM hash serialization
- LC27. WLM serialization latch for stored procedures/user-defined functions
- LC32. Storage manager serialization
- IRLM. IRLM hash contention
- CML. z/OS Cross-memory local suspend lock
- UTSERIAL. Utility serialization lock for SYSLGRNG (NFM)

Logging performance is enhanced in DB2 10. Log synchronous writes performance is improved. In some scenarios, DB2 logging suspension time drops by 50 percent compared with DB2 9. DB2 10 log asynchronous writes performance changes, in combination with disk storage enhancements, help increase logging asynchronous throughput that benefits massive batch processing.

All these improvements have the potential to reduce the elapsed time required by batch processing. Batch jobs might end sooner after migration to DB2 10. Having the overnight processing end sooner provides an additional buffer before the opening of the OLTP window. This extra buffer can sometimes compensate for unexpected peaks in batch processing, seasonal treatments, or operational problems during night processing.

The value of this extra buffer is difficult to measure in financial terms. Nevertheless, it can help avoid service disruptions and delays, which are quantifiable depending on the activity. The extra buffer can provide a better quality of service, increasing customer satisfaction.

DB2 Storage and Scalability

The addressable storage below the 2 GB bar, also known as *BTB*, has been the scalability limit of DB2 for z/OS in many scenarios. At a glance, the available storage BTB limits the number of concurrent threads that a single DB2 subsystem can handle. DB2 for z/OS has been improving its scalability with each new release by moving internal structures from BTB to above the bar. Figure 33 summarizes this evolution.

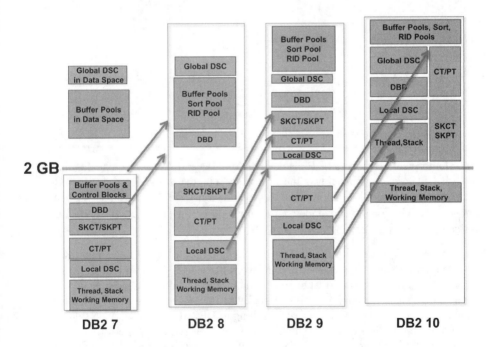

Figure 33: DB2 storage scalability evolution

Before DB2 10, a safe number of concurrent threads per DB2 subsystem was counted as a few hundred. Although recent DB2 versions have made improvements in this area, virtual storage BTB remains the most common constraint. This constraint is commonly known as Virtual Storage Constraint (VSC).

DB2 10 for z/OS provides a significant step forward in scalability by moving a large portion (from 50 to 90 percent) of the BTB storage to 64-bit virtual storage. These benefits are available to dynamic SQL immediately after migrating to DB2 10. Static SQL using packages will benefit after a REBIND.

Figure 34 compares the DB2 storage BTB between DB2 9 and DB2 10 for the same workload. The DB2 10 memory changes substantially increase the number of concurrent threads that can be supported by a single DB2 subsystem. DB2 10 has the potential to support five to ten times more concurrent users and up to 20,000 concurrent users in a single DB2 subsystem.

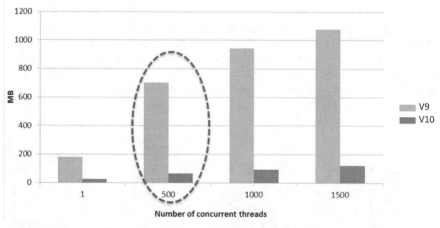

Figure 34: DB2 storage (DBM1) below the 2 GB bar

Memory enhancements BTB also allows for BIND and REBIND options that may provide CPU reduction benefits at the expense of a bigger thread footprint. This CPU versus storage tradeoff, which was not affordable before DB2 10, becomes a performance opportunity. These options include a larger utilization of RELEASE(DEALLOCATE) and larger MAXKEEPD values for KEEPDYNAMIC=YES.

Nevertheless, storage enhancements BTB comes at the expense of higher overall real storage requirements. That is, for the same workload, DB2 10 uses a lot less memory BTB, but it may require up to 10 to 30 percent more real storage. *Real storage* refers to the actual physical memory available in the LPAR. Over-commitment of real storage, which could just be a consequence of migrating to DB2 10, will result in system paging. System paging is a less desirable situation and may degrade LPAR performance overall. To an extent, virtual storage BTB concerns before DB2 10 may translate to real storage concerns after DB2 10. The monitoring focus shifts from virtual to real storage. Fortunately, the acquisition cost of real storage has been dropping substantially with the latest System z generation of servers.

IMPORTANT: DB2 11 continues this trend by further moving DB2 structures from BTB to above the bar.
